¡VIVA!

Edexcel GCSE (9–1) Spanish
Foundation
Vocabulary Book

Pearson

Published by Pearson Education Limited, 80 Strand, London, WC2R 0RL
www.pearsonschoolsandfecolleges.co.uk
Text © Pearson Education Limited 2017
Editorial management by Gwladys Rushworth for Haremi
Edited by Ruth Manteca
Typeset by York Publishing Solutions Pvt. Ltd.
Cover image: Alamy Images: Kevin George
Cover © Pearson Education Limited 2017

Written by Penny Fisher

First published 2017
10 9 8 7

British Library Cataloguing in Publication Data
A catalogue record for this book is available from the British Library.
ISBN 978 1 292 17259 0

Copyright notice
All rights reserved. No part of this publication may be reproduced in any form or by any means (including photocopying or storing it in any medium by electronic means and whether or not transiently or incidentally to some other use of this publication) without the written permission of the copyright owner, except in accordance with the provisions of the Copyright, Design and Patents Act 1988 or under the terms of a license issued by the Copyright Licensing Agency, Barnard's Inn, 86 Fetter Lane, London EC4A 1EN (www.cla.co.uk). Applications for the copyright owner's written permission should be addressed to the publisher.

Printed in the UK by Ashford Colour Press

Contenidos

High-frequency words 4

Módulo 1
Words I should know for speaking and writing activities 13
Extra words I should know for reading and listening activities 16

Módulo 2
Words I should know for speaking and writing activities 17
Extra words I should know for reading and listening activities 20

Módulo 3
Words I should know for speaking and writing activities 21
Extra words I should know for reading and listening activities 24

Módulo 4
Words I should know for speaking and writing activities 25
Extra words I should know for reading and listening activities 29

Módulo 5
Words I should know for speaking and writing activities 30
Extra words I should know for reading and listening activities 33

Módulo 6
Words I should know for speaking and writing activities 34
Extra words I should know for reading and listening activities 37

Módulo 7
Words I should know for speaking and writing activities 38
Extra words I should know for reading and listening activities 41

Módulo 8
Words I should know for speaking and writing activities 42
Extra words I should know for reading and listening activities 45

High-frequency words

Common verbs

alcanzar	to reach
abrir	to open
cerrar	to close
comenzar	to begin
continuar	to continue
corregir	to correct
dar	to give
dejar de	to stop (doing something)
echar	to throw
empezar	to begin
estar equivocado/a	to make a mistake / to be wrong
hacer	to do / to make
ir	to go
irse	to go away / to leave
mentir	to tell a lie
necesitar	to need
permitir	to allow
poner	to put
ponerse a	to start doing something
prohibir	to forbid / to ban
seguir	to continue / to follow
tener	to have / to own
tener razón	to be right

Had a look ☐ Nearly there ☐ Nailed it ☐

acabar de + infinitive	to have just (done something)
deber	to must / to have to
estar	to be
hace(n) falta	to need / to be necessary
hacerse	to become
hay	there is / there are
hay que	one must / one has to
ir a + infinitive	(to be) going to (do something)
poder	to be able / can
ser	to be
soler + infinitive	to regularly do (something)
tener que + infinitive	to have to do (something)
volver a + infinitive	to do (something) again
volverse	to become

Had a look ☐ Nearly there ☐ Nailed it ☐

bastar	to be enough
durar	to last
estar situado/a	to be situated
encontrarse	to be situated
hace (+ time) …	it's been …
medir	to measure
mojar(se)	to get wet
ocurrir	to happen
pasar	to happen / to go through / to spend (time)

pesar	to weigh
tener (calor / frío)	to feel (hot / cold)
tener lugar	to take place
tener prisa	to be in a hurry
valer la pena	to be worth the trouble

Had a look ☐ Nearly there ☐ Nailed it ☐

adorar	to adore / to love
alegrar	to cheer up
alegrarse (de)	to be happy about
apreciar	to appreciate
aprovechar	to make the most
aprovecharse (de)	to take advantage (of)
desear	to wish
disfrutar	to enjoy
divertirse	to have a good time
encantar	to delight
estar a favor de	to be in favour of
estar de acuerdo	to agree
pasarlo bien / mal	to have a good / bad time
querer	to want / to love
sentir(se)	to feel

Had a look ☐ Nearly there ☐ Nailed it ☐

creer	to believe
darse cuenta (de)	to realise
decidir	to decide
decir	to say
dudar	to doubt
esperar	to hope
opinar	to think / to give an opinion
parecer	to seem
pensar	to think
ponerse de acuerdo	to agree
preferir	to prefer
quedar en	to agree
querer decir	to mean
reconocer	to recognise
saber	to know (a fact / how to do something)
tener razón	to be right

Had a look ☐ Nearly there ☐ Nailed it ☐

aburrirse	to get bored
decepcionar	to disappoint
dar igual	to be all the same / to make no difference
estar en contra	to be against
estar harto/a de	to be fed up with
fastidiar	to annoy / to bother
odiar	to hate

Had a look ☐ Nearly there ☐ Nailed it ☐

High-frequency words

Common adjectives

afortunado/a	lucky	caro/a	expensive
agradable	pleasant	cierto/a	certain / sure / true
alucinante	amazing	distinto/a	different
bonito/a	pretty	duro/a	hard
bueno/a	good	equivocado/a	wrong
divertido/a	amusing / entertaining	fácil	easy
emocionante	exciting / thrilling / moving	gratis / gratuito/a	free (of charge)
encantador(a)	charming	libre	free / unoccupied
entretenido/a	entertaining / amusing	lento/a	slow
espléndido/a	fantastic / great / terrific	mediano/a	medium
estupendo/a	fantastic / marvellous	ocupado/a	engaged / occupied
fenomenal	great / fantastic	profundo/a	deep / profound
genial	brilliant / great	raro/a	strange / rare
guay	cool	seguro/a	safe / certain / self-assured
hermoso/a	beautiful	sencillo/a	simple / plain / straightforward
maravilloso/a	marvellous	sorprendido/a	surprised
impresionante	impressive / striking	tranquilo/a	peaceful / quiet
increíble	incredible	único/a	unique / only / single
precioso/a	precious / beautiful	útil	useful

Had a look ☐ Nearly there ☐ Nailed it ☐   Had a look ☐ Nearly there ☐ Nailed it ☐

aburrido/a	boring / bored		
decepcionado/a	disappointed	**Common adverbs**	
decepcionante	disappointing	afortunadamente	fortunately
desagradable	unpleasant	bien	well
fatal	awful / fatal	casi	almost
horroroso/a	horrible	deprisa	quickly
inseguro	unsafe / uncertain / insecure	desafortunadamente	unfortunately
		desgraciadamente	unfortunately
inútil	useless	especialmente	especially
malo/a	bad	inmediatamente	immediately
		mal	badly

Had a look ☐ Nearly there ☐ Nailed it ☐

		más	more
		no obstante	nevertheless
abierto/a	open	por suerte	fortunately
alto/a	tall / high	quizás / quizá	perhaps
ancho/a	wide	rápidamente	quickly
antiguo/a	old	realmente	really
bajo/a	low / short	recientemente	recently
cerrado/a	closed	sin embargo	nevertheless
delgado/a	slim / thin	sobre todo	especially
estrecho/a	narrow		

Had a look ☐ Nearly there ☐ Nailed it ☐

feo/a	ugly
gordo/a	fat
grueso/a	thick
lleno/a	full
nuevo/a	new
tonto/a	silly
vacío/a	empty
viejo/a	old

Prepositions

a	to / at
de	from / of
en	in
hacia	towards
hasta	until
para	for
por	through / by / in / for / per
según	according to
sin	without

Had a look ☐ Nearly there ☐ Nailed it ☐

apropiado/a	correct / appropriate
barato/a	cheap

Had a look ☐ Nearly there ☐ Nailed it ☐

High-frequency words

Connectives
además	moreover / besides
aparte de	apart from
claro que	of course
dado que	given that
es decir	in other words / that is to say
por un lado ... por otro lado	on the one hand ... on the other hand
por una parte ... por otra parte	on the one hand ... on the other hand
sin duda	obviously / certainly / undoubtedly
incluso	even
mientras (que)	while / meanwhile
o/u	or
pero	but
por eso	for that reason / therefore
por lo tanto	therefore
porque	because
pues	then / since
si	if
sin embargo	however
tal vez	maybe / perhaps
también	also
ya que	as / since

Had a look ☐ Nearly there ☐ Nailed it ☐

Negatives
jamás	never
ni ... ni	neither ... nor
nada	nothing
nadie	nobody
ninguno/a	none / no one / any / no
nunca	never
sino	but / except
tampoco	neither / not ... either ...
ya no	not any more

Had a look ☐ Nearly there ☐ Nailed it ☐

Comparisons / Superlatives
bastante	sufficient / enough / quite
demasiado/a	too / too much
igual que	same as
más (que)	more (than)
mayor	main / major / larger / bigger / greater
la mayoría	most / majority
mejor	better / best
menor	smaller / less / least
menos (que)	less (than)
mismo/a	same
muy	very
parecido/a a	like / similar to
peor	worse / worst
poco (ruidoso)	not very (noisy)
tan ... como	as ... as
tanto/a ... como	as much ... as

Had a look ☐ Nearly there ☐ Nailed it ☐

Conjunctions
a pesar de	in spite of / despite
así que	so / therefore
aun (cuando)	even (if)
aunque	although / (even) though
como	as / since
cuando	when

Question words
¿(a)dónde?	where?
¿cómo?	how?
¿cuál(es)?	which?
¿cuándo?	when?
¿cuánto/a?	how much?
¿cuántos/as ...?	how many?
¿de dónde?	where from?
¿de quién?	whose?
¿por dónde?	through where?
¿por qué?	why?
¿qué?	what?
¿quién?	who?

Had a look ☐ Nearly there ☐ Nailed it ☐

¿a qué hora?	at what time?
¿cuánto cuesta(n)?	how much does it / do they cost?
¿cuánto es?	how much is it?
¿cuánto vale(n)?	how much does it / do they cost?
¿cuántos años tiene(s)?	how old are you?
¿de qué color?	what colour?
¿para / por cuánto tiempo?	for how long?
¿qué día?	what day?
¿qué fecha?	what date?
¿qué hora es?	what time is it?

Had a look ☐ Nearly there ☐ Nailed it ☐

Time expressions
a la una	at one o'clock
a las dos / etc.	at two o'clock / etc.
y cinco / etc.	five past / etc.
y cuarto	quarter past
y media	half past
menos cuarto	quarter to
menos diez / etc.	ten to / etc.
de la mañana	in the morning

High-frequency words

de la tarde	in the afternoon / in the evening
es la una	it's one o'clock
son las dos / etc.	it's two o'clock / etc.
la hora	hour
el minuto	minute
la medianoche	midnight
el mediodía	noon

Had a look ☐ **Nearly there** ☐ **Nailed it** ☐

el año	year
anoche	last night
ayer	yesterday
el día	day
el fin de semana	weekend
el mes	month
la estación	season
esta noche	tonight
hoy	today
la fecha	date
la mañana	morning
la noche	night
la semana	week
la tarde	afternoon / evening
mañana	tomorrow
pasado mañana	day after tomorrow
quince días	fortnight
el rato	while / short time
el pasado	past
el porvenir	future

Had a look ☐ **Nearly there** ☐ **Nailed it** ☐

Days / months and seasons of the year

lunes	Monday
martes	Tuesday
miércoles	Wednesday
jueves	Thursday
viernes	Friday
sábado	Saturday
domingo	Sunday
(el) lunes	(on) Monday
(el) lunes por la mañana	(on) Monday morning
(el) lunes por la tarde	(on) Monday evening
los lunes	on Mondays
cada lunes	every Monday

Had a look ☐ **Nearly there** ☐ **Nailed it** ☐

enero	January
febrero	February
marzo	March
abril	April
mayo	May
junio	June
julio	July
agosto	August
septiembre	September
octubre	October
noviembre	November
diciembre	December

Had a look ☐ **Nearly there** ☐ **Nailed it** ☐

la primavera	spring
el verano	summer
el otoño	autumn
el invierno	winter

Had a look ☐ **Nearly there** ☐ **Nailed it** ☐

Frequency expressions

a diario	daily / everyday
a eso de …	at about …
a mediados de …	around the middle of …
a menudo	often
a partir de	from
a veces	sometimes
ahora	now / nowadays
al mismo tiempo	at the same time
algunas veces	sometimes
antes (de)	before
cada (…) días / horas	every (…) days / hours
de vez en cuando	now and then / from time to time
dentro de (…) días / horas	within (…) days / hours
desde / desde hace	since
después (de)	after / afterwards
durante	during
en seguida / enseguida	straightaway
entonces	then
luego	then / afterwards
mientras tanto	meanwhile

Had a look ☐ **Nearly there** ☐ **Nailed it** ☐

de momento	at the moment / right now
de nuevo	again
otra vez	again
de repente	suddenly
(por) mucho tiempo	(for) a long time
pocas veces	seldom / a few times
por fin	at last
al principio	at the beginning
pronto	soon
próximo/a	next
que viene (el mes / etc.)	next (month / etc.)
siempre	always
siguiente	next / following
sobre	on / around
tarde	late
temprano	early

High-frequency words

todos/as (las semanas / los días / meses)	*every (week / day / month)*		
todavía	*still / yet*		
último/a	*last*		
una vez (dos / tres veces / etc.)	*once (twice / three times / etc.)*		
ya	*already*		

Had a look ☐ **Nearly there** ☐ **Nailed it** ☐

Location and distance

abajo (de)	*under / below*
afuera (de)	*outside*
ahí	*there*
allá	*over there*
allí	*over there*
atrás	*behind*
delante (de)	*in front of*
detrás (de)	*behind*
cerca (de)	*near*
enfrente (de)	*opposite*
entre	*between*
a la derecha / izquierda	*on the / to the right / left*
a mano derecha / izquierda	*on the right / left*
a un paso (de)	*a few steps away*
al final (de)	*at the end of*
al lado (de)	*next to*
en la esquina	*on the corner*
todo recto	*straight on / ahead*

Had a look ☐ **Nearly there** ☐ **Nailed it** ☐

alrededor (de)	*around*
aquí	*here*
arriba (de)	*above / on top (of)*
cercano/a	*nearby*
contra	*against*
debajo (de)	*under*
dentro (de)	*inside*
en el medio (de)	*in the middle of*
en / por todas partes	*everywhere*
en las afueras	*in the outskirts*
encima (de)	*above / on top / overhead*
el este	*east*
en el / al fondo	*at the back / at the bottom*
fuera (de)	*outside*
lejos (de)	*far (from)*
el lugar	*place*
el norte	*north*
el oeste	*west*
el sitio	*place*
el sur	*south*

Had a look ☐ **Nearly there** ☐ **Nailed it** ☐

Numbers

uno	1
dos	2
tres	3
cuatro	4
cinco	5
seis	6
siete	7
ocho	8
nueve	9
diez	10
once	11
doce	12
trece	13
catorce	14
quince	15
dieciséis	16
diecisiete	17
dieciocho	18
diecinueve	19
veinte	20

Had a look ☐ **Nearly there** ☐ **Nailed it** ☐

veintiuno	21
veintidós	22
veintitrés	23
veinticuatro	24
veinticinco	25
veintiséis	26
veintisiete	27
veintiocho	28
veintinueve	29
treinta	30

Had a look ☐ **Nearly there** ☐ **Nailed it** ☐

cuarenta	40
cincuenta	50
sesenta	60
setenta	70
ochenta	80
noventa	90
cien(to)	100
ciento uno/a	101
doscientos/as	200
mil	1,000
mil cien(to)	1,100
dos mil	2,000
(un) millón (de)	1,000,000

Had a look ☐ **Nearly there** ☐ **Nailed it** ☐

primer / primero/a	*first*
segundo/a	*second*

High-frequency words

tercer / tercero/a	third
cuarto/a	fourth
quinto/a	fifth
sexto/a	sixth
séptimo/a	seventh
octavo/a	eighth
noveno/a	ninth
décimo/a	tenth

Had a look ☐ Nearly there ☐ Nailed it ☐

mil novecientos noventa y cinco	1995
dos mil diecisiete	2017
(una) docena	dozen
el número	number
un par	pair / couple
unos/as (diez)	about (10)

Had a look ☐ Nearly there ☐ Nailed it ☐

Colours

amarillo/a	yellow
azul	blue
blanco/a	white
castaño/a	chestnut brown
claro/a	light
el color	colour
gris	grey
marrón	brown
morado/a / violeta	purple / violet
moreno/a	dark (hair / skin)
naranja	orange
negro	black
oscuro/a	dark
pálido/a	pale
rojo/a	red
rosa / rosado/a	pink
rubio/a	fair (hair / skin)
verde	green
vivo/a	vivid / bright

Had a look ☐ Nearly there ☐ Nailed it ☐

Weather

el cielo	sky
el clima	climate
el chubasco	shower
la lluvia	rain
la niebla	fog
la nieve	snow
la nube	cloud
el pronóstico	forecast
el relámpago	lightning
el grado	degree
el hielo	ice
el tiempo	weather
la tormenta	storm
el trueno	thunder
el viento	wind

Had a look ☐ Nearly there ☐ Nailed it ☐

caliente	hot
caluroso	hot / warm
despejado	clear (skies)
estable	stable / steady / unchanged
fresco	fresh
húmedo	humid
nublado / nuboso	cloudy
seco	dry
la sombra	shade / shadow
templado	mild / temperate
tormentoso	stormy
buen / mal tiempo	good / bad weather
hacer (frío / calor / etc.)	to be (cold / hot / etc.)
helar	to freeze
llover	to rain
mojar(se)	to get wet
nevar	to snow
tener (calor / frío)	to feel (hot / cold)

Had a look ☐ Nearly there ☐ Nailed it ☐

Weights, measures and containers

la altura	height
el ancho / la anchura	width
la bolsa	bag
el bote	jar
la caja	box
la cantidad	quantity
el cartón	carton
un cuarto	quarter
la lata	tin
la medida	measure
medio	half
la mitad	half
el pedazo	piece
el peso	weight
un poco	little
la ración	portion
la talla	size (clothes)
el tamaño	size
el trozo	piece

Had a look ☐ Nearly there ☐ Nailed it ☐

Countries and continents

Alemania	Germany
Austria	Austria
Bélgica	Belgium
Dinamarca	Denmark

High-frequency words

Escocia	Scotland	sueco/a	Swedish
España	Spain	suizo/a	Swiss
Francia	France	turco/a	Turkish
Gran Bretaña	Great Britain		
Grecia	Greece		
Holanda	Holland		

Had a look ☐ Nearly there ☐ Nailed it ☐

Inglaterra	England	americano/a	American
Irlanda	Ireland	argentino/a	Argentinian
Italia	Italy	boliviano/a	Bolivian
(País de) Gales	Wales	brasileño/a	Brazilian
Países Bajos	Netherlands	chileno/a	Chilean
Reino Unido	United Kingdom	chino/a	Chinese
Suecia	Sweden	colombiano/a	Colombian
Suiza	Switzerland	ecuatoriano/a	Ecuadorean
Turquía	Turkey	indio/a	Indian
		italiano/a	Italian

Had a look ☐ Nearly there ☐ Nailed it ☐

		japonés/japonesa	Japanese
		mexicano/a	Mexican
Argentina	Argentina	pakistaní	Pakistani
Brasil	Brazil	peruano/a	Peruvian
Estados Unidos	United States	ruso/a	Russian
India	India	venezolano/a	Venezuelan
México	Mexico		

Had a look ☐ Nearly there ☐ Nailed it ☐

Pakistán	Pakistan
Perú	Peru
Rusia	Russia

Had a look ☐ Nearly there ☐ Nailed it ☐

Areas / mountains and seas

Andalucía	Andalusia
Aragón	Aragon
el canal de la Mancha	the English Channel
Castilla	Castile
Cataluña	Catalonia
comunidades autónomas	autonomous communities
Galicia	Galicia
el mar Cantábrico	Cantabrian Sea
el mar Mediterráneo	Mediterranean Sea
el océano Atlántico	Atlantic Ocean
(el) País Vasco	(the) Basque Country
los Pirineos	the Pyrenees
La Rioja	Rioja

África	Africa
América del Norte / Norteamérica	North America
América del Sur / Sudamérica	South America
América Latina / Latinoamérica	Latin America
Asia	Asia
Australia	Australia
Europa	Europe

Had a look ☐ Nearly there ☐ Nailed it ☐

Had a look ☐ Nearly there ☐ Nailed it ☐

Nationalities

alemán/alemana	German
austriaco/a	Austrian
belga	Belgian
británico/a	British
danés/danesa	Danish
escocés/escocesa	Scottish
español/a	Spanish
europeo/a	European
francés/francesa	French
galés/galesa	Welsh
griego/a	Greek
holandés/holandesa	Dutch
inglés/inglesa	English
irlandés/irlandesa	Irish
italiano/a	Italian

Materials

el algodón	cotton
la cerámica	pottery
el cristal	glass / crystal
el cuero	leather
la lana	wool
la madera	wood
el oro	gold
el papel	paper
la piel	leather / skin
la plata	silver
la seda	silk
la tela	fabric / material
el vidrio	glass

Had a look ☐ Nearly there ☐ Nailed it ☐

High-frequency words

Greetings and exclamations

¿Cómo está(s)?	How are you?
¿De veras?	Really?
con permiso	excuse me
de nada	you're welcome / don't mention it
encantado/a	pleased to meet you
hasta el (lunes)	till / see you (Monday)
hasta luego	see you later
hasta mañana	see you tomorrow
hasta pronto	see you soon
lo siento	I'm sorry
mucho gusto	pleased to meet you
perdón	sorry
perdone	sorry
por favor	please
¡Que lo pase(s) bien!	Have a good time!
¿Qué hay?	What's happening? / What's the matter?
¿Qué pasa?	What's happening? / What's the matter?
¿Qué tal?	How are you? / How's …?
saludar	to greet / to say hello
saludos	regards / greetings
vale	OK

Had a look ☐ **Nearly there** ☐ **Nailed it** ☐

¡Basta ya!	That's enough!
¡Bienvenido/a!	Welcome!
¡Buen viaje!	Have a good trip!
¡Buena suerte!	Good luck!
¡Claro!	Of course!
¡Cuidado!	Careful! / Watch out!
¡Enhorabuena!	Congratulations!
¡Felices vacaciones!	Have a good holiday!
¡Felicidades!	Best wishes! / Congratulations!
¡Felicitaciones!	Congratulations!
¡Ojo!	Watch out! / Careful!
¡Qué (+ adjective)!	How …!
¡Qué (+ noun)!	What a …!
¡Que suerte!	What luck!
¡Qué va!	Come on! / Rubbish! / Nonsense!
¡Socorro!	Help!

Had a look ☐ **Nearly there** ☐ **Nailed it** ☐

Language used in dialogues and messages

a la atención de	for the attention of
el auricular	receiver (telephone)
con relación a	further to / following
de momento	at the moment
en contacto con	in communication with
enviado/a por	sent by
escucho / dígame	I'm listening
espere	wait
hablando / al aparato / en la línea	on the line / speaking
le paso	I will put you through
llámame (informal) / llámeme (formal)	call me (informal / formal)
marcar el número	dial the number
el mensaje (de texto)	text message
el mensaje en el contestador	voice mail
no cuelgue	stay on the line
el número equivocado	wrong number
el prefijo	area code
el teléfono	telephone
el texto	text
el timbre / el tono	tone
vuelvo enseguida	I'll be right back

Had a look ☐ **Nearly there** ☐ **Nailed it** ☐

Other useful expressions

aquí lo tiene(s)	here you are
buena suerte	good luck
¿Cómo se escribe?	How do you spell that?
con (mucho) gusto / placer	with pleasure
de acuerdo	OK (I agree)
depende	it depends
en mi opinión	in my opinion
estoy bien	I'm fine
gracias	thank you
he tenido bastante	I've had enough
me da igual	I don't mind
menos mal	just as well
mío/a	mine
no importa	it doesn't matter
otra vez	once again
por supuesto	of course
por si acaso	just in case
qué lástima / qué pena	what a shame
ten (informal) / tenga (formal)	there you are (informal / formal)

Had a look ☐ **Nearly there** ☐ **Nailed it** ☐

Other useful words

algo	something
alguien	someone
la cifra	figure
como	as / like
la cosa	thing
la desventaja	disadvantage
el mundo	everybody
todos	everybody
eso/a/os/as	that / those
esto/a/os/as	this / these

Had a look ☐ **Nearly there** ☐ **Nailed it** ☐

High-frequency words

la falta	*error*
la forma	*shape*
la forma	*way*
la manera	*way*
el género	*type / kind / sort*
el tipo	*type / kind / sort*
el medio	*middle*
la mitad	*half*
no	*no*
el número	*number*
por ejemplo	*for example*
la razón	*reason*
señor	*Mr*
señora	*Mrs*
señorita	*Miss*
si	*if*
sí	*yes*
la ventaja	*advantage*
la verdad	*truth*

Had a look ☐ **Nearly there** ☐ **Nailed it** ☐

Módulo 1 Palabras

Words I should know for speaking and writing activities

¿Qué haces en verano?
Compro un montón de revistas.
Escucho música / la radio.
Hago deporte / kárate / los deberes / submarinismo.
Juego a los videojuegos / al baloncesto / al voleibol.
Monto a caballo / en bici.
Nado en el mar.
Salgo con mis amigos / mi hermano/a.
Toco la guitarra / el piano.
Veo la tele / un partido de fútbol.
Voy al parque / a la playa / al centro comercial.

What do you do in summer?
I buy loads of magazines.
I listen to music / the radio.
I do sport / karate / homework / diving.
I play computer games / basketball! / volleyball.
I go horseriding / cycling.
I swim in the sea.
I go out with my friends / my brother / sister.
I play the guitar / the piano.
I watch TV / a football match.
I go to the park / to the beach / to the shopping centre.

Had a look ☐   Nearly there ☐   Nailed it ☐

¿Con qué frecuencia?
siempre
a menudo
todos los días
a veces
una vez a la semana
dos o tres veces a la semana
casi nunca
nunca
Cuando …
hace buen tiempo
hace mal tiempo
hace calor / hace frío
hace sol / hace viento
llueve / nieva

How often?
always
often
every day
sometimes
once a week
two or three times a week
almost never
never
When …
it's good weather
it's bad weather
it's hot / cold
it's sunny / windy
it's raining / snowing

Had a look ☐   Nearly there ☐   Nailed it ☐

¿Cómo prefieres pasar las vacaciones?
¿Dónde vives?
Vivo en el …
norte / sur …
este / oeste …
de España / México
de Inglaterra / Escocia
de Gales / Irlanda (del Norte)

How do you prefer to spend the holidays?
Where do you live?
I live in the …
north / south …
east / west …
of Spain / Mexico
of England / Scotland
of Wales / (Northern) Ireland

Tengo … semanas de vacaciones.
Soy adicto/a a …
Soy un(a) fanático/a de …
ya que / dado que
Prefiero …
Me gusta …
Me encanta / Me mola / Me chifla …
No me gusta (nada) …
Odio …

I have … weeks holiday.
I'm addicted to …
I'm a … fan / fanatic
given that / since
I prefer …
I like …
I love …
I don't like … (at all)
I hate …

Had a look ☐   Nearly there ☐   Nailed it ☐

A (mi padre) le gusta …
estar al aire libre
hacer artes marciales / deportes acuáticos
ir de compras / de excursión
leer
no hacer nada
tomar el sol
usar el ordenador
ver películas

(My dad) likes …
being outdoors
doing martial arts / water sports
going shopping / on an excursion
reading
doing nothing
sunbathing
using the computer
watching films

Had a look ☐   Nearly there ☐   Nailed it ☐

Mis vacaciones ideales
Prefiero ir de vacaciones en …
primavera / verano / otoño / invierno
Me gusta ir a la costa / al campo / a la montaña / a la ciudad
Prefiero ir a un hotel / un camping / un apartamento / una casa rural
Es divertido / barato / interesante / relajante

My ideal holidays
I prefer going on holiday in …
spring / summer / autumn / winter
I like going to the coast / countryside / mountains / city
I prefer going to a hotel / campsite / apartment / house in the country
It's fun / cheap / interesting / relaxing

Had a look ☐   Nearly there ☐   Nailed it ☐

¿Adónde fuiste de vacaciones?
Hace una semana / un mes
Hace dos semanas / meses / años
El año / verano pasado
Fui de vacaciones a …
Francia / Italia / Turquía
¿Con quién fuiste?

Where did you go on holiday?
A week / month ago
Two weeks / months / years ago
Last year / summer
I went on holiday to …
France / Italy / Turkey
Who did you go with?

13

Módulo 1 Palabras

Fui …	I went …
con mi familia / insti	with my family / school
con mi mejor amigo/a	with my best friend
solo/a	alone
¿Cómo viajaste?	How did you travel?
Viajé …	I travelled …
en autocar / avión	by coach / plane
en barco / coche / tren	by boat / car / train

Had a look ☐ Nearly there ☐ Nailed it ☐

¿Qué hiciste? / *What did you do?*

primero	first
luego	then
después	after
más tarde	later
finalmente	finally

Had a look ☐ Nearly there ☐ Nailed it ☐

Lo mejor / peor fue cuando …	The best / worst thing was when …
aprendí a hacer vela	I learned to sail
comí muchos helados	I ate lots of ice creams
compré recuerdos	I bought souvenirs
descansé	I rested
hice esquí / turismo / windsurf	I went skiing / sightseeing / windsurfing
perdí mi móvil	I lost my mobile phone
saqué fotos	I took photos
tomé el sol	I sunbathed
tuve un accidente en la playa	I had an accident on the beach
vi un partido en el estadio	I saw / watched a match at the stadium
visité el Park Güell	I visited Park Güell
visité … a pie / en bici / en Segway	I visited … on foot / by bike / by Segway
vomité en una montaña rusa	I was sick on a roller coaster
fuimos al Barrio Gótico	we went to the gothic quarter
vimos los barcos en el puerto	we saw the boats in the port
visitamos el Museo Picasso	we visited the Picasso Museum

Had a look ☐ Nearly there ☐ Nailed it ☐

¿Qué tal lo pasaste? / *How was it?*

Lo pasé fenomenal / fatal	I had a great / awful time
Lo pasé bien / mal	I had a good / bad time
En mi opinión / Creo que …	In my opinion / I think that …
Fue inolvidable / interesante / flipante / horroroso	It was unforgettable / interesting / awesome / awful
¡Qué aburrido / miedo / guay!	How boring / scary / cool!
¡Qué desastre!	What a disaster!
¿Qué tiempo hizo?	What was the weather like?
Hizo buen / mal tiempo.	It was good / bad weather.
Hizo calor / frío.	It was hot / cold.
Hizo sol / viento.	It was sunny / windy.
Llovió / Nevó.	It rained / It snowed.
excepto el martes, cuando …	except for Tuesday, when …

Had a look ☐ Nearly there ☐ Nailed it ☐

¿Dónde te alojaste? / *Where did you stay?*

Me alojé / Me quedé …	I stayed …
en un albergue juvenil / un hotel	in a youth hostel / a hotel
en un parador	in a state-run luxury hotel
en un camping / una pensión	on a campsite / in a guest house
Estaba …	It was …
cerca de la playa	near the beach
en el centro de la ciudad	in the city centre
en el campo	in the country
¿Cómo era el hotel?	What was the hotel like?
Era …	It was …
un poco / bastante …	a little bit / quite …
muy / demasiado …	very / too …
antiguo/a	old
animado/a	lively
barato/a	cheap
caro/a	expensive
cómodo/a	comfortable
grande	big
lujoso/a	luxurious
moderno/a	modern
pequeño/a	small
ruidoso/a	noisy
tranquilo/a	quiet

Had a look ☐ Nearly there ☐ Nailed it ☐

Tenía …	It had …
Había …	There was/were …
No tenía ni … ni …	It had neither … nor …
Además, no tenía …	Furthermore, it didn't have …
(un) bar	a bar
(un) gimnasio	a gym
(un) restaurante	a restaurant
(una) cafetería	a café
(una) discoteca	a disco
(una) piscina climatizada	a heated pool
(una) sauna	a sauna
mucho espacio	lots of space

Had a look ☐ Nearly there ☐ Nailed it ☐

Módulo 1 Palabras

Quisiera reservar ...	***I would like to book ...***
¿Hay ...	Is/Are there ...
aire acondicionado?	air conditioning?
aparcamiento?	parking?
wifi gratis?	free wifi?
(una) tienda de recuerdos?	a gift shop?
¿Cuánto cuesta una habitación ...?	How much does a ... room cost?
Son ... euros por noche.	It's ... euros per night.
¿A qué hora se sirve el desayuno?	What time is breakfast served?
¿Cuándo está abierto/a el/la ...?	When is the ... open?
¿Hasta qué hora está abierto el/la ...?	What time is the ... open until?
¿Se admiten mascotas?	Are pets allowed?
Hay un suplemento para perros.	There's a supplement for dogs.

Had a look ☐ **Nearly there** ☐ **Nailed it** ☐

Quisiera reservar ...	I would like to book ...
una habitación individual / doble	a single / double room
con / sin balcón	with / without a balcony
con baño / ducha	with a bath / shower
con vistas al mar	with a sea view
con cama de matrimonio	with a double bed
con desayuno	with breakfast
con media pensión	with half board
con pensión completa	with full board
¿Para cuántas noches?	For how many nights?
Para ... noches	For ... nights
del ... al ... de ...	from the ... to the ... of ...

Had a look ☐ **Nearly there** ☐ **Nailed it** ☐

Quiero quejarme	***I want to complain***
Quiero ...	I want ...
hablar con el director.	to speak to the manager.
cambiar de habitación.	to change room.
un descuento.	a discount.
El aire acondicionado ...	The air conditioning ...
El ascensor ...	The lift ...
La ducha ...	The shower ...
La habitación ...	The room ...
La luz ...	The light ...
no funciona.	doesn't work.
está sucio/a.	is dirty.
Hay ratas en la cama.	There are rats in the bed.
No hay ...	There is no ...

Had a look ☐ **Nearly there** ☐ **Nailed it** ☐

Necesito ...	I need ...
papel higiénico	toilet paper
jabón / champú	soap / shampoo
toallas / (un) secador	towels / a hairdryer
¿Cuál es el problema?	What's the problem?
¿Qué habitación es?	Which room is it?
¿Cómo se llama usted?	What are you called? (polite)
¿Cómo se escribe?	How do you spell that?
¿Puede repetir, por favor?	Can you repeat, please?

Had a look ☐ **Nearly there** ☐ **Nailed it** ☐

Mis vacaciones desastrosas	***My disastrous holiday***
Por lo general	In general
Por un lado ... por otro lado ...	On one hand ... on the other hand ...
Sin embargo	However
Por eso	Therefore / So
El primer día / último día ...	(On) the first / last day ...
Al día siguiente ...	On the following day ...

Had a look ☐ **Nearly there** ☐ **Nailed it** ☐

alquilé una bicicleta	I hired a bicycle
conocí a mucha gente	I met lots of people
fui a una fiesta	I went to a festival / party
perdí mis gafas de sol	I lost my sunglasses
visité el pueblo	I visited the town / village
cogimos el teleférico	we took the cable car
decidimos acampar	we decided to camp
fuimos de excursión	we went on an excursion
Tuve / Tuvimos ...	I had / We had ...
un retraso / una avería.	a delay / a breakdown.
Tuve / Tuvimos que ...	I had to / We had to ...
ir a la comisaría.	go to the police station.
llamar a un mecánico.	call a mechanic.
Perdí / Perdimos ...	I lost / We lost ...
el equipaje / la cartera / las llaves.	the luggage / the wallet / the keys.
El paisaje era precioso.	The landscape was beautiful.

Had a look ☐ **Nearly there** ☐ **Nailed it** ☐

15

Módulo 1 Palabras

Extra words I should know for reading and listening activities

¡Desconéctate y pásalo bien!	Switch off and have a good time!
la actividad deportiva	sports activity
los adictos a la adrenalina	people who get a kick from an adrenaline rush
Apúntate a un taller de cocina italiana.	Sign up for an Italian cookery course.
el baile	dancing
el bañador	swimming costume
bañarse	to bathe / to swim
el barco	boat
la crema solar	suncream
el dibujo	drawing
encantador(a)	charming
la estación de esquí	ski station
al / en el extranjero	abroad
inscribirse (en un curso)	to enroll yourself (on a course)
ir de pesca	to go fishing
(una) manera rápida y fácil de visitar la ciudad	(a) quick and easy way to visit the city

Had a look ☐ **Nearly there** ☐ **Nailed it** ☐

navegar por Internet	to surf the (inter)net
el país	country
el paraguas*	umbrella
la pintura	painting
la pista de esquí	ski slope
preparar espaguetis / lasañas / pizzas	to prepare / make spaghetti / lasagna / pizza
el/la principiante	beginner
relajarse	to relax
la sierra	mountains
sin coste	free

Had a look ☐ **Nearly there** ☐ **Nailed it** ☐

Recomendaciones	Recommendations
tomar precauciones	to take precautions
Limitar las horas al sol.	Don't spend too much time in the sun.
Beber un mínimo de ... al día.	Drink a minimum of ... a day.
No perder de vista los objetos de valor.	Don't lose sight of / Keep an eye on things of value.
No comer justo antes de nadar en el mar.	Don't eat just before you go swimming in the sea.

Had a look ☐ **Nearly there** ☐ **Nailed it** ☐

El alojamiento**	Accommodation
alquilado/a	rented
alquilar un apartamento	to rent an apartment
el ambiente	atmosphere
el aseo	bathroom / WC / toilet
el baño	bathroom / bath
la calefacción	heating
el campamento de verano	summer camp
construido/a	built
el cuarto de baño	bathroom
el descuento	discount
el dormitorio	bedroom
la ducha	shower
el edificio emblemático	emblematic building
el hotel de calidad	a top hotel
el hotel de cinco estrellas	five-star hotel

Had a look ☐ **Nearly there** ☐ **Nailed it** ☐

las instalaciones	facilities
la habitación	room
el lavabo	washbasin
limpio/a	clean
la maleta	suitcase
el parador	luxury hotel (usually in a historic building)
el precio	price
¡Qué incómodo/a!	How uncomfortable!
la recepción	reception
la reserva	reservation
la segunda residencia	second home

Had a look ☐ **Nearly there** ☐ **Nailed it** ☐

⭐ ***Work out the meaning of unfamiliar words using clues**
When trying to work out the meaning of a word look for clues. *El paraguas* combines the words *para* and *agua*, which would literally translate 'for water'. Note too that although *paraguas* ends with 's' it is a singular noun so you would say, for example, ¿*Dónde está mi paraguas?*

⭐ ****Work out meanings of new words drawing on what you already know**
Another way to work out the meaning of a new word is to ask yourself if it is similar to one you already know. For example, if you know that *alojarse* means 'to stay', it's not difficult to work out that in the phrase *En términos de alojamiento, la opción preferida es ir a un hotel*, the word *alojamiento* means 'accommodation / place to stay'.

Módulo 2 Palabras

Words I should know for speaking and writing activities

¿Te interesa(n)…?	Are you interested in…?
el arte dramático	drama
el dibujo	art / drawing
el español	Spanish
el inglés	English
la biología	biology
la educación física	PE
la física	physics
la geografía	geography
la historia	history
la informática	ICT
la lengua	language
la química	chemistry
la religión	RE
la tecnología	technology
los idiomas	languages
las empresariales	business studies
las matemáticas	maths
las ciencias	science
la asignatura	subject

Had a look ☐   Nearly there ☐   Nailed it ☐

¿Qué opinas de …?	What do you think of …?
me encanta(n)	I love
me chifla(n)	I love
me interesa(n)	I'm interested in
me gusta(n)	I like
no me gusta(n)	I don't like
odio	I hate
prefiero	I prefer

Had a look ☐   Nearly there ☐   Nailed it ☐

¿Cómo son tus profes?	What are your teachers like?
Mi profe (de inglés) es …	My (English) teacher is …
joven	young
viejo/a	old
severo/a	strict
tolerante	easy-going
impaciente	impatient
paciente	patient
interesante	interesting
aburrido/a	boring
gracioso/a	funny
serio/a	serious
simpático/a	nice / friendly
antipático/a	unfriendly
más divertido/a que	more fun than
menos creativo/a que	less creative than
tan interesante como	as interesting as

Had a look ☐   Nearly there ☐   Nailed it ☐

¿Qué llevas en el insti?	What do you wear at school?
(No) llevo …	I (don't) wear …
(No) llevamos …	We (don't) wear …
Tengo que llevar …	I have to wear …
Tenemos que llevar …	We have to wear …
un jersey (de punto)	a (knitted) sweater
un vestido	a dress
una camisa	a shirt
una camiseta	a t-shirt
una chaqueta (a rayas)	a (striped) jacket
una chaqueta de punto	a cardigan
una corbata	a tie
una falda	a skirt
unos pantalones	trousers
unos calcetines	socks
unos zapatos	shoes
unos vaqueros	jeans
unas medias	tights

Had a look ☐   Nearly there ☐   Nailed it ☐

amarillo/a	yellow
blanco/a	white
negro/a	black
rojo/a	red
morado / violeta	purple
naranja	orange
rosa	pink
azul	blue
verde	green
gris	grey
marrón	brown

Had a look ☐   Nearly there ☐   Nailed it ☐

oscuro / claro	dark / light
a rayas / a cuadros	striped / checked
bonito / feo	pretty / ugly
cómodo / incómodo	comfortable / uncomfortable
formal / informal	formal / informal
elegante	smart
práctico	practical
El uniforme …	Uniform …
mejora la disciplina	improves discipline
limita la individualidad	limits individuality
Las diferencias económicas no son tan obvias.	The economic differences are not as obvious.

Had a look ☐   Nearly there ☐   Nailed it ☐

¿Cómo es tu insti?	What is your school like?
En mi insti hay …	In my school there is …
Mi insti tiene …	My school has …
un salón de actos	a hall

Módulo 2 Palabras

un comedor	a canteen
un campo de fútbol	a football pitch
un patio	a playground
un gimnasio	a gym
una piscina	a pool
una biblioteca	a library
una pista de tenis	a tennis court
unos laboratorios	some laboratories
muchas aulas	lots of classrooms

Had a look ☐ **Nearly there** ☐ **Nailed it** ☐

Mi instituto / colegio es …	My school is …
mixto	mixed
femenino / masculino	all girls / all boys
público / privado	state / private
El edificio es …	The building is …
Los edificios son …	The buildings are …
nuevo(s)	new
antiguo(s)	old
moderno(s)	modern
amplio(s)	spacious
pequeño(s)	small
feo(s)	ugly
atractivo(s)	attractive
lo bueno / malo es que …	the good / bad thing is that …
lo mejor / peor es que …	the best / worst thing is that …
ni … ni …	(n)either … nor …
nada	nothing / anything
tampoco	not either

Had a look ☐ **Nearly there** ☐ **Nailed it** ☐

En mi escuela primaria …	In my primary school …
(no) había …	there was/were (not any) …
exámenes	exams
deberes	homework
instalaciones (deportivas)	(sports) facilities
actividades extraescolares	extra-curricular activities
la educación infantil	pre-school education
la educación primaria	primary education
la educación secundaria	secondary education
el bachillerato	A levels
la formación profesional	vocational training
el instituto	secondary school

Had a look ☐ **Nearly there** ☐ **Nailed it** ☐

¿Cómo vas al insti?	**How do you get to school?**
Voy al insti …	I go to school …
a pie / andando	on foot / walking
en bici	by bike
en autobús	by bus
en coche	by car
en metro	by underground
en taxi	by taxi
en tren	by train
Salgo de casa a las …	I leave home at …
Las clases empiezan a las …	Lessons start at …
y terminan a las …	and finish at …
Tenemos … clases al día	We have … lessons per day
por la mañana	in the morning
por la tarde	in the afternoon
Cada clase dura …	Each lesson lasts …
el recreo	break
la hora de comer	lunch

Had a look ☐ **Nearly there** ☐ **Nailed it** ☐

¿Cuáles son las normas de tu insti?	**What are the rules in your school?**
Está prohibido …	It is forbidden …
No se permite …	You are not allowed …
No se debe …	You / One must not …
comer chicle	chew chewing gum
usar el móvil en clase	use your phone in lessons
llevar uniforme	wear a uniform
ser agresivo o grosero	be aggressive or rude
correr en los pasillos	run in the corridors
llevar piercings	have visible piercings
ser puntual	be on time
salir del instituto durante el día escolar	leave the school during the school day

Had a look ☐ **Nearly there** ☐ **Nailed it** ☐

estoy de acuerdo	I agree
no estoy de acuerdo	I disagree
En mi opinión, …	In my opinion, …
Pienso que / Creo que …	I think that …
es justo	it's fair
es injusto	it's unfair
no es justo	it's not fair
¡Qué va!	No way!
Las normas son …	The rules are …
buenas / malas	good / bad
necesarias	necessary
demasiado severas	too strict

Had a look ☐ **Nearly there** ☐ **Nailed it** ☐

¿Hay problemas en tu insti?	**Are there problems in your school?**
Un problema es …	One problem is …
el estrés de los exámenes	exam stress
el acoso escolar	bullying
la presión del grupo	peer pressure

Módulo 2 Palabras

Estoy estresado/a.	I am stressed out.
Tengo miedo de …	I am scared of …
suspender mis pruebas.	fail(ing) my assessments
aprobar mis exámenes	pass(ing) my exams
Hay (algunos) alumnos que …	There are (some) pupils who …
intimidan	intimidate
abusan	abuse
sienten pánico	feel panic
hacen novillos	skip lessons
quieren ser parte de la pandilla	want to be part of the gang
son una mala influencia	are a bad influence

Had a look ☐ **Nearly there** ☐ **Nailed it** ☐

¿Qué vas a hacer?	**What are you going to do?**
Voy a …	I'm going to …
Vamos a …	We're going to …
participar en un intercambio	take part in an exchange
viajar con mi clase	travel with my class
conocer	meet / get to know
visitar	visit
llegar	arrive
estar	be
asistir a clases	attend lessons
ir a pie	walk
llevar ropa de calle	wear (my / your / our) own clothes
ir / comer juntos	go / eat together
ir de excursión	go on a trip
hacer turismo	see the sights
hacer una visita guiada	do a guided tour
ver los edificios	see the buildings
Va a ser …	It's going to be …
fácil / guay	easy / cool

Had a look ☐ **Nearly there** ☐ **Nailed it** ☐

Éxitos	**Successes / Achievements**
practico el judo	I do / have been doing judo
toco la trompeta	I play / have been playing the trumpet
canto en el coro	I sing / have been singing in the choir
voy al	I go to / I have been going to
club de (ajedrez)	(chess) club
Soy miembro del …	I am / have been a member of the …
club de teatro	drama club
club de periodismo	reporters clubs
club de lectores	reading club
club de fotografía	photography club
desde hace …años	for … years
el trimestre pasado …	last term …
participé en …	I took part in …
un maratón	a marathon
un torneo	a tournament
un concierto	a concert
un campeonato	a championship
un concurso	a competition

Had a look ☐ **Nearly there** ☐ **Nailed it** ☐

hice / hicimos …	I / we did …
una prueba	a test / exam
una película	a film
gané / ganamos …	I won / we won …
un trofeo	a trophy
un premio	a prize
toqué un solo	I played a solo
¡Fue un éxito!	It was a success!
este trimestre …	this term …
el próximo trimestre	next term …
voy a continuar con …	I'm going to continue with …
voy a ir al club de …	I'm going to go to … club
Los clubs extraescolares …	Extra-curricular clubs …
son divertidos / geniales / interesantes	are fun / great / interesting
Te ayudan a …	They help you to …
aprender cosas interesantes	learn interesting things
hacer nuevos amigos	make new friends

Had a look ☐ **Nearly there** ☐ **Nailed it** ☐

Módulo 2 Palabras

Extra words I should know for reading and listening activities

Lo que hacemos en el insti	**What we do at school**
bailar	*to dance*
conocer	*to meet / to know*
contestar	*to answer*
entender	*to understand*
escuchar	*to listen to*
explicar	*to explain*
faltar	*to be absent*
fracasar	*to fail*
llegar pronto / tarde	*to arrive early / late*
mejorar	*to improve*
(no) ser bueno/a en algo	*(not) to be good at something*
preguntar	*to ask*
repasar	*to revise*
respetar	*to respect / to take care of*
sacar buenas / malas notas	*to get good / bad marks / grades*
ser imaginativo/a	*to be imaginative*
suspender	*to fail*
terminar	*to finish*
tocar un instrumento*	*to play an instrument*
pasar lista	*to call the register*

Had a look ☐ Nearly there ☐ Nailed it ☐

Lo que hay en el insti	**What there is in school**
el alemán	German
el comercio	business studies
el/la compañero/a	classmate
la cocina	food technology / cookery
el inglés	English
el equipo	team
el francés	French
la obra de teatro	play
el periodismo	journalism
el/la periodista	journalist
la pista de atletismo	athletics track
la regla	rule

el resumen	*summary*
la reunión	*meeting*
la rutina de baile	*dance routine*
la sala de profesores	*staffroom*
el salón de actos	*hall / assembly room*
el taller de baile	*dance workshop*
el tema	*topic*
los vestuarios	*changing rooms*

Had a look ☐ Nearly there ☐ Nailed it ☐

Expresiones y descripciones	**Expressions and descriptions**
bien equipado/a	*well-equipped*
bienvenido/a**	*welcome*
confundido/a	*confused*
desobediente	*disobedient*
duro/a	*hard / difficult*
obligatorio/a	*compulsory*
el sentido del humor	*sense of humour*
sobresaliente	*outstanding*
superdivertido/a	*really fun*
superfácil	*very easy*
superfeo/a	*really ugly*
Fue un éxito.	*It was a success.*
Quiero mantener mi propia individualidad.	*I want to maintain my own individuality.*

Had a look ☐ Nearly there ☐ Nailed it ☐

⭐ ***Learn and use the right verbs**
'To play an instrument' in Spanish is *tocar un instrumento*. Don't fall into the trap of using the verb *jugar*.
Note too that the spelling of the 'I' form in the preterite changes, for example: *Ayer toqué el piano*. Yesterday I played the piano.

⭐ ****Break unfamiliar words down to work out their meaning**
If you know the meanings of component parts of unfamiliar words and phrases, you can often work out what they mean. So for example the component parts of *bienvenido* are:
bien well
venido the past participle of *venir* (to come)

Words I should know for speaking and writing activities

¿Qué aplicaciones usas?	What apps do you use?
Uso … para …	I use … (in order) to …
subir y ver vídeos	upload and watch videos
compartir fotos	share photos
pasar el tiempo	pass the time
organizar las salidas con mis amigos	organise to go out with my friends
contactar con mi familia	contact my family
descargar música	download music
chatear	chat
aprender idiomas	learn languages
controlar mi actividad física	monitor my physical activity
publicar mensajes	post messages

Had a look ☐ Nearly there ☐ Nailed it ☐

Es / No es …	It is / It isn't …
cómodo/a	handy / convenient
divertido/a	fun
peligroso/a	dangerous
práctico/a	practical
rápido/a	quick
fácil de usar	easy to use
popular	popular
útil	useful
gratis	free
adictivo/a	addictive
mi red social preferida	my favourite social network
una pérdida de tiempo	a waste of time
la mejor app	the best app
Estoy enganchado/a a …	I am hooked on …

Had a look ☐ Nearly there ☐ Nailed it ☐

¿Qué estás haciendo?	What are you doing?
Estoy …	I am …
tocando la guitarra	playing the guitar
hablando por teléfono	talking on the phone
jugando con mi móvil	playing on my phone
comiendo pizza	eating pizza
tomando el sol	sunbathing
esperando a …	waiting for …
viendo una peli	watching a film
leyendo	reading
durmiendo	sleeping
escribiendo	writing
pensando en salir	thinking of going out
actualizando mi página de Facebook	updating my Facebook page
editando mis fotos	editing my photos

Had a look ☐ Nearly there ☐ Nailed it ☐

¿Quieres salir conmigo?	Do you want to go out with me?
No puedo porque …	I can't because …
está lloviendo	it's raining
tengo que …	I have to …
visitar a (mi abuela)	visit (my grandmother)
cuidar a (mi hermano)	look after (my brother)
quiero …	I want …
subir mis fotos	to upload my photos
quedarme en casa	to stay at home
dar una vuelta	to go for a wander
¡Qué pena!	What a shame!
¿A qué hora quedamos?	What time shall we meet?
¿Dónde quedamos?	Where shall we meet?
En la plaza Mayor.	In the main square.
Vale	OK

Had a look ☐ Nearly there ☐ Nailed it ☐

¿Qué te gusta leer?	What do you like reading?
los tebeos / los cómics	comics
los periódicos	newspapers
las revistas	magazines
las novelas de ciencia ficción	science fiction novels
las novelas de amor	romantic novels
las historias de vampiros	vampire stories
las biografías	biographies

Had a look ☐ Nearly there ☐ Nailed it ☐

¿Con qué frecuencia lees?	How often do you read?
todos los días	every day
a menudo	often
de vez en cuando	from time to time
una vez a la semana	once a week
dos veces al mes	twice a month
una vez al año	once a year
nunca	never
un ratón de biblioteca	a bookworm
un(a) fan del manga	a manga fan

Had a look ☐ Nearly there ☐ Nailed it ☐

¿Qué es mejor, e-books o libros en papel?	What is better, e-books or paper books?
Los e-books …	E-books …
cuestan menos que los libros tradicionales	cost less than traditional books
son más …	are more …
transportables	portable

Módulo 3 Palabras

ecológicos	environmentally-friendly
cansan la vista	tire your eyes
usan batería	use battery
Las páginas ...	The pages ...
no tienen números	don't have numbers
una ventaja	an advantage
una desventaja	a disadvantage
Leer en formato digital ...	Reading in digital format ...
protege el planeta	protects the planet
es más barato	is cheaper
depende de la energía eléctrica	depends on electricity

Had a look ☐ **Nearly there** ☐ **Nailed it** ☐

La familia / Family

el padre	father
la madre	mother
el padrastro	step-father
la madrastra	step-mother
el hermano	brother
la hermana	sister
el hermanastro	step-brother
la hermanastra	step-sister
el abuelo	grandfather
la abuela	grandmother

Had a look ☐ **Nearly there** ☐ **Nailed it** ☐

el tío	uncle
la tía	aunt
el primo	male cousin
la prima	female cousin
el sobrino	nephew
la sobrina	niece
el marido	husband
la mujer	wife
el hijo	son
la hija	daughter
el nieto	grandson
la nieta	granddaughter
mayor	older
menor	younger

Had a look ☐ **Nearly there** ☐ **Nailed it** ☐

¿Cómo es? / What is he/she like?

Tiene los ojos ...	He/She has ... eyes
azules	blue
verdes	green
marrones	brown
grises	grey
grandes	big
pequeños	small
Tiene el pelo ...	He/She has ... hair
moreno	dark-brown
castaño	mid-brown / chestnut
rubio	blond
rojo	red
corto	short
largo	long
rizado	curly
liso	straight
ondulado	wavy
Tiene ...	He/She has ...
pecas	freckles

Had a look ☐ **Nearly there** ☐ **Nailed it** ☐

Lleva ...	He/She wears ...
gafas	glasses
barba	a beard
bigote	a moustache
Es ...	He/She is ...
alto/a	tall
bajo/a	short
delgado/a	slim
gordito/a	chubby
gordo/a	fat
calvo/a	bald
moreno/a	dark-haired
rubio/a	fair-haired
castaño/a	brown-haired
pelirrojo/a	red-haired
No es ni gordo/a ni delgado/a	He/She is neither fat nor thin

Had a look ☐ **Nearly there** ☐ **Nailed it** ☐

¿Cómo es de carácter? / What is he/she like as a person?

Como persona, es ...	As a person, he/she is ...
optimista	optimistic
pesimista	pessimistic
trabajador(a)	hard-working
perezoso/a	lazy
hablador(a)	chatty
tímido/a	shy
divertido/a	fun
serio/a	serious
gracioso/a	funny
generoso/a	generous
fiel	loyal

Had a look ☐ **Nearly there** ☐ **Nailed it** ☐

Módulo 3 Palabras

¿Te llevas bien con tu familia y tus amigos? *Do you get on well with your family and friends?*

Me llevo bien con … — *I get on well with …*
No me llevo bien con … — *I don't get on well with …*
Me divierto con … — *I have a good time with …*
Me peleo con … — *I argue with …*

Had a look ☐ **Nearly there** ☐ **Nailed it** ☐

¿Cómo es un buen amigo / una buena amiga? *What is a good friend like?*

Un buen amigo / Una buena amiga es alguien que … — *A good friend is someone who …*
te ayuda — *helps you*
te apoya — *supports you*
te conoce bien — *knows you well*
te acepta — *accepts you*
te hace reír — *makes you laugh*
te dice la verdad — *tells you the truth*
Conocí a … — *I met …*
mi mejor amigo/a — *my best friend*
hace (cuatro) años — *(four) years ago*
tenemos mucho en común — *we have a lot in common*

Had a look ☐ **Nearly there** ☐ **Nailed it** ☐

Módulo 3 Palabras

Extra words I should know for reading and listening activities

Describiendo a una persona	Describing someone
¿Cómo es físicamente?	What does he/she look like?
¿Cómo es de carácter?	What is he/she like?
alegre	happy
amable	kind
amistoso/a	friendly
anciano/a	(very) old
el/la anciano/a	old person
animado/a	lively
antipático/a	unpleasant
el aspecto	appearance / looks
la cara	face
cariñoso/a	affectionate
la felicidad	happiness
feliz*	happy
el/la hijo/a único/a	only child
el/la joven	young person
simpático/a	friendly
triste	sad

Had a look ☐ Nearly there ☐ Nailed it ☐

Relaciones de pareja	Partnerships
el amor	love
el bebé	baby
la boda	wedding
casado/a	married
el champán	champagne
echar de menos	to miss
enamorarse	to fall in love
los hijos	children
la novia	girlfriend / bride
el novio	boyfriend / groom
la pareja ideal	ideal partner
el pastel de boda	wedding cake

Had a look ☐ Nearly there ☐ Nailed it ☐

Otras palabras y frases útiles	Other useful words and phrases
buscar (información)	to look for (information)
charlar	to chat
disfrutar de algo	to enjoy something
en mis ratos libres	in my free time
escribir anotaciones	to write notes
escuchar música	to listen to music
estar en contacto con	to be in contact with
hablar por Skype	to talk on Skype
Leer es un placer.	Reading is a pleasure.
mandar SMS / mensajes	to send texts / messages
mostrar	to show
nacer	to be born

Had a look ☐ Nearly there ☐ Nailed it ☐

las noticias	the news
la numeración de páginas	page numbering
ocupar espacio	to take up space
el ordenador	computer
los parientes**	relatives
¿Puede decirle …?	Can you tell him/her …?
el punto de encuentro	meeting point
recargar	to recharge
señalar algo con el dedo	to point at something with your finger
sonreír	to smile

Had a look ☐ Nearly there ☐ Nailed it ☐

⭐ ***Agreement of adjectives**
Don't forget that adjectives have to agree with the nouns they are describing. However, in the case of *feliz*, note that there is no change of ending to agree with masculine or feminine singular nouns, and the masculine and feminine forms in the plural are the same, but the **z** in the singular changes to a **c**, for example:

un niño feli**z**   unos niños feli**c**es
una niña feli**z**   unas niñas feli**c**es

⭐ ****Watch out for false friends**
Be aware that *los parientes* means 'relatives' not 'parents'. Look at the two sentences below:
Vivo con mis padres. I live with my **parents**.
No tengo muchos parientes. I don't have many **relatives**.

Words I should know for speaking and writing activities

La paga — Pocket money
Recibo ... — I receive ...
... euros a la semana / al mes — ... euros a week / a month
dinero de vez en cuando — money from time to time
dinero para mi cumpleaños — money for my birthday
Gasto mi paga en ... — I spend my pocket money on ...
Compro ... — I buy ...
caramelos — sweets
saldo para el móvil — credit for my mobile phone
revistas — magazines
videojuegos — computer games
ropa y maquillaje — clothes and make up

Had a look ☐ Nearly there ☐ Nailed it ☐

Mis ratos libres — My freetime
Tengo muchos pasatiempos. — I have lots of hobbies.
A la hora de comer ... — At lunchtime ...
Cuando tengo tiempo ... — When I have time ...
Después del insti ... — After school ...
Los fines de semana ... — At weekends ...
Los (lunes) ... — On (Mondays) ...
Por la mañana ... — In the morning ...
Por la tarde ... — In the afternoon / evening ...
Por la noche ... — At night ...

Had a look ☐ Nearly there ☐ Nailed it ☐

cocino — I cook
juego al futbolín / al squash — I play table football / squash
monto en bici / monopatín — I ride my bike / skateboard
toco la guitarra / trompeta — I play the guitar / trumpet
voy / vamos ... — I go / we go ...
al polideportivo — to the sports centre
al centro comercial — to the shopping centre
a la pista de hielo — to the ice rink
a la bolera — to the bowling alley
Suelo ... — I tend to / I usually ...
descansar — rest
escuchar música / la radio — listen to music / the radio
hacer deporte — do sport
ir al cine — go to the cinema
leer libros / revistas / periódicos — read books / magazines / newspapers

salir con amigos — go out with friends
usar el ordenador — use the computer
ver la tele — watch TV

Had a look ☐ Nearly there ☐ Nailed it ☐

Es divertido / sano — It's fun / healthy
Soy ... — I am ...
activo/a — active
creativo/a — creative
sociable — sociable
adicto/a a ... — addicted to ...
Me hace reír / relajarme — It makes me laugh / relax
Necesito estar ... — I need to be ...
al aire libre — outdoors
en contacto con otra gente — in touch with other people

Had a look ☐ Nearly there ☐ Nailed it ☐

La música — Music
Me gusta ... — I like ...
el soul — soul
el rap — rap
el dance — dance
el hip-hop — hip-hop
el pop — pop
el rock — rock
el jazz — jazz
la música clásica — classical music
la música electrónica — electronic music

Had a look ☐ Nearly there ☐ Nailed it ☐

Toco ... — I play
Mi hermano / hermana toca ... — My brother / sister plays ...
el teclado — the keyboard
el piano — the piano
la batería — the drums
la flauta — the flute
Mi cantante favorito/a es ... — My favourite singer is ...
Fui a un concierto de ... — I went to a ... concert.
Canté y bailé. — I sang and danced.
Compré una camiseta de la gira. — I bought a tour t-shirt.
Comí ... — I ate ...
Bebí ... — I drank ...
Fue genial / increíble / inolvidable. — It was great / incredible / unforgettable.

Had a look ☐ Nearly there ☐ Nailed it ☐

Módulo 4 Palabras

25

Módulo 4 Palabras

El deporte	Sport
Antes era …	Before I used to be …
Ahora soy …	Now I am …
(bastante / muy) deportista	(quite / very) sporty
miembro de un club / un equipo	a member of a club / a team
aficionado/a de …	a fan of …
un(a) fanático/a de …	a … fanatic
Juego al …	I play …
Jugué al …	I played …
Jugaba al …	I used to play …
baloncesto	basketball
balonmano	handball
críquet	cricket
fútbol	football
hockey	hockey
ping-pong	table tennis
rugby	rugby
tenis	tennis
voleibol	volleyball

Had a look ☐ Nearly there ☐ Nailed it ☐

Hago …	I do …
Hice …	I did …
Hacía …	I used to do …
atletismo	athletics
ciclismo	cycling
equitación	horseriding
escalada	climbing
gimnasia	gymnastics
judo	judo
kárate	karate
natación	swimming
patinaje sobre hielo	ice skating
piragüismo	canoeing
Ya no (juego) …	(I) no longer (play) …
Entreno	I train

Had a look ☐ Nearly there ☐ Nailed it ☐

Ayer …	Yesterday …
Esta mañana …	This morning …
La temporada pasada …	Last season …
jugué un partido	I played a match
marqué un gol	I scored a goal
gané / ganamos el campeonato	I / we won the championship
Mi jugador(a) favorito/a es …	My favourite player is …
Lo mejor fue cuando …	The best thing was when …
batió el récord	he/she beat the record
ganó / marcó …	he/she won / scored …

Had a look ☐ Nearly there ☐ Nailed it ☐

La tele	TV
(No) soy teleadicto/a	I'm (not) a TV addict
Veo la tele … horas al día	I watch TV … hours a day
Mi programa favorito es …	My favourite programme is …
un concurso	a game / quiz show
un programa de deporte	a sports programme
un reality	a reality TV show
un documental	a documentary
una telenovela	a soap
una comedia	a comedy
una serie policíaca	a crime series

Had a look ☐ Nearly there ☐ Nailed it ☐

Me gustan las comedias	I like comedies
No me gustan las noticias	I don't like the news
Es / Son …	It is / They are …
aburrido/a(s)	boring
adictivo/a(s)	addictive
divertido/a(s)	fun
entretenido/a(s)	entertaining
tonto/a(s)	silly
informativo/a(s)	informative
emocionante(s)	exciting
interesante(s)	interesting

Had a look ☐ Nearly there ☐ Nailed it ☐

Las películas	Films
una película de amor	a love film
una película de terror	a horror film
una película de acción	an action film
una película de aventuras	an adventure film
una película de animación	an animated film
una película de ciencia ficción	a sci-fi film
una película de fantasía	a fantasy film
una película extranjera	a foreign film

Had a look ☐ Nearly there ☐ Nailed it ☐

Nacionalidades	Nationalities
americano/a	American
británico/a	British
griego/a	Greek
italiano/a	Italian
mexicano/a	Mexican
alemán/alemana	German
español(a)	Spanish
francés/francesa	French
galés/galesa	Welsh
inglés/inglesa	English

Módulo 4 Palabras

irlandés/irlandesa	Irish	¿En el cine o en casa?	At the cinema or at home?
japonés/japonesa	Japanese	Prefiero ir al cine porque …	I prefer going to the cinema because …

Had a look ☐ **Nearly there** ☐ **Nailed it** ☐

Temas del momento / *Trending topics*

He compartido …	I have shared …
He comprado …	I have bought …
He descargado …	I have downloaded …
He gastado …	I have spent …
He hecho …	I have done …
He jugado …	I have played …
He leído …	I have read …
He perdido …	I have lost …
He subido …	I have uploaded …
He visto …	I have seen / watched …
el nuevo álbum / libro de …	the new … album / book
la nueva canción / película de …	the new … song / film

Prefiero ver las pelis en casa porque … / *I prefer watching films at home because …*
el ambiente es mejor. / *the atmosphere is better.*
la imagen es mejor en la gran pantalla. / *the picture is better on the big screen.*
los asientos no son cómodos. / *the seats aren't comfortable.*
los otros espectadores me molestan. / *the other spectators annoy me.*
las entradas son caras. / *the tickets are expensive.*
las palomitas están ricas. / *the popcorn is tasty.*
hay demasiadas personas. / *there are too many people.*
me encanta ver los tráilers para las nuevas pelis. / *I love watching the trailers for the new films.*
(No) estoy de acuerdo. / *I (don't) agree.*

Had a look ☐ **Nearly there** ☐ **Nailed it** ☐

Had a look ☐ **Nearly there** ☐ **Nailed it** ☐

Ir al cine, al teatro, etc. / *Going to the cinema, theatre, etc.*

¿Qué música has escuchado …	What music have you listened to …
esta semana / este mes / este año?	this week / this month / this year?
Cuenta la historia de …	It tells the story of …
Combina el misterio con la acción.	It combines mystery with action.
El final …	The ending …
La banda sonora …	The soundtrack …
es bueno/a / malo/a	is good / bad
es feliz / triste / raro/a	is happy / sad / strange
Los actores …	The actors …
Los gráficos …	The graphics …
Los efectos especiales …	The special effects …
Los personajes …	The characters …
Las animaciones …	The animations …
Las canciones …	The songs …
son …	are …
buenos/as	good
estupendos/as	brilliant
decepcionantes	disappointing
guapos/as	good looking
interesantes	interesting
irritantes	irritating
impresionantes	impressive
locos/as	mad
originales	original

¿Tienes ganas de ir … / *Do you fancy going …*
a un festival? / *to a festival?*
a un espectáculo de …? / *to a … show?*
al cine / al teatro / al circo? / *to the cinema / theatre / circus?*
esta tarde? / *this afternoon / evening?*
esta noche? / *tonight?*
mañana? / *tomorrow?*
el viernes? / *on Friday?*
¿Qué ponen? / *What's on?*
Es una película / obra de … / *It's a … film / play.*
¿Cuánto cuesta? / *How much does it cost?*
Son … euros. / *It's … euros.*
¿A qué hora empieza / termina? / *What time does it start / finish?*
Empieza a las … / *It starts at …*
Termina a las … / *It finishes at …*
Dos entradas para …, por favor. / *Two tickets for …, please.*
Para la sesión de las … / *For the … showing / performance.*
No quedan entradas. / *There are no tickets left.*

Had a look ☐ **Nearly there** ☐ **Nailed it** ☐

Had a look ☐ **Nearly there** ☐ **Nailed it** ☐

M4

Módulo 4 Palabras

Los modelos a seguir *Role models*

Mi modelo a seguir es …	*My role model is …*
Admiro a … porque …	*I admire … because …*
ayuda a organizaciones benéficas	*he/she helps charities*
lucha por / contra …	*he/she fights for / against …*
la pobreza	*poverty*
los derechos humanos	*human rights*
tiene mucho talento / éxito	*he/she is very talented / successful*
tiene mucha determinación	*he/she has a lot of determination*
trabaja en defensa de los animales	*he/she works in defence of animals*
usa su fama para ayudar a otros	*he/she uses his/her fame to help others*

Had a look ☐ **Nearly there** ☐ **Nailed it** ☐

Es …	*He/She is …*
No es ni … ni …	*He/She is neither … nor …*
ambicioso/a	*ambitious*
egoísta	*selfish*
famoso/a	*famous*
fuerte	*strong*
generoso/a	*generous*
optimista	*optimistic*
rico/a	*rich*
simpático/a	*nice*
trabajador(a)	*hardworking*
valiente	*brave*
Ha batido muchos récords.	*He/She has beaten lots of records.*
Ha ganado muchos premios.	*He/She has won lots of prizes / awards.*
Ha hablado abiertamente de …	*He/She has spoken openly about …*
Ha hecho varias películas.	*He/She has made several films.*
Ha recaudado más de …	*He/She has raised more than …*
Ha sufrido varias enfermedades.	*He/She has suffered several illnesses.*
Ha superado sus problemas.	*He/She has overcome his/her problems.*

Had a look ☐ **Nearly there** ☐ **Nailed it** ☐

Extra words I should know for reading and listening activities

Verbos útiles	*Useful verbs*
adorar	to adore / to love
añadir	to add
correr	to run
hacer footing	to go jogging
inspirar a	to inspire
intervenir	to intervene
marcar (un gol)*	to score (a goal)
murmurar	to murmur / to mutter
nadar	to swim
patinar	to skate
recomendar	to recommend
ser aficionado/a a	to be very keen on / fond of (activity)
sobrevivir	to survive
suspirar	to sigh

Had a look ☐   Nearly there ☐   Nailed it ☐

Nombres útiles	*Useful nouns*
la actriz principal	main actress
el baile	dancing
el campeón / la campeona	winner / champion
la canción	song
el carné de estudiante	student card
la carrera**	race / career / degree
la copa	cup / trophy
la corrida de toros	bull fight
el/la deportista	sportsman / sportswoman
los dibujos animados	cartoons
la entrada	ticket
el espectáculo	show
el estadio	stadium
el estilo libre	crawl / free style (swimming)
el estreno	new release

Had a look ☐   Nearly there ☐   Nailed it ☐

el héroe anónimo	unsung hero
el juego	game / fun / amusement
los Juegos Olímpicos	Olympic Games
la letra	words (of song)
el/la mejor actor/ actriz / director(a)	best actor / director
el/la nadador(a)	swimmer
el ocio	leisure
la pantalla gigante	giant screen
el papel	role
la pelota	ball
la pista	track / court / run / slope / rink
los poderes mágicos	magic powers
el recuerdo	memory
el tiempo libre	free time
el torneo	tournament
la vela	sail / sailing
la voz	voice

Had a look ☐   Nearly there ☐   Nailed it ☐

Expresiones y adjetivos	*Expressions and adjectives*
¡Es un crack!	He's a real champion!
apto/a	suitable
de alta calidad	high-quality
en directo	live
hermoso/a	lovely / beautiful
me ayuda a (relajarme)	it helps me (to relax)
multijugador(a)	multiplayer
no hay nada mejor que (hacer algo)	there's nothing better than (doing something)
parecido/a a	similar to

Had a look ☐   Nearly there ☐   Nailed it ☐

---

*Learn irregular verb forms and spelling changes
Remember that *marcar* is one of the verbs in which the spelling changes for the 'I form' of the preterite, for example:
Marco muchos goles cuando juego al fútbol. I score lots of goals when I play football.
El sábado pasado marqué un gol. Last Saturday I scored a goal.

**Some words have more than one meaning
Use the context to get the correct meaning of some words that have more than one meaning. For example, *una carrera* can mean 'a race', 'a degree' or 'a career'. Look at the following sentences:
Gané la carrera de bicis. I won the bike race.
No quiero tener niños porque mi carrera es muy importante. I don't want to have any children because my career is very important.
Estoy haciendo la carrera de medicina. I'm studying medicine for my degree.

Módulo 5 Palabras

Words I should know for speaking and writing activities

En mi ciudad / *In my town*

Hay ...	*There is / are ...*
un ayuntamiento	*a town hall*
un bar / muchos bares	*a bar / lots of bars*
un castillo	*a castle*
un cine	*a cinema*
un centro comercial	*a shopping centre*
un mercado	*a market*
un museo / unos museos	*a museum / a few museums*
un parque	*a park*
un polideportivo	*a sports centre*
un puerto	*a port*

Had a look ☐ Nearly there ☐ Nailed it ☐

muchos restaurantes	*lots of restaurants*
un teatro	*a theatre*
una biblioteca	*a library*
una bolera	*a bowling alley*
una iglesia	*a church*
una piscina	*a swimming pool*
una playa / unas playas	*a beach / a few beaches*
una plaza Mayor	*a town square*
una pista de hielo	*an ice rink*
(una oficina de) Correos	*a post office*
una tienda / muchas tiendas	*a shop / lots of shops*
(No) hay mucho que hacer.	*There is (not) a lot to do.*

Had a look ☐ Nearly there ☐ Nailed it ☐

Vivo en un pueblo ...	*I live in a ... village*
Vivo en una ciudad ...	*I live in a ... town*
histórico/a	*historic*
moderno/a	*modern*
tranquilo/a	*quiet*
ruidoso/a	*noisy*
turístico/a	*touristy*
industrial	*industrial*
bonito/a	*pretty*
feo/a	*ugly*
Está en ...	*It is in ...*
el norte	*the north*
el sur	*the south*
el este	*the east*
el oeste	*the west*
del país	*of the country*

Had a look ☐ Nearly there ☐ Nailed it ☐

¿Por dónde se va al / a la...? / *How do you get to the...?*

¿Dónde está el / la ...?	*Where is the ...?*
¿Para ir al / a la ...?	*How do I get to the ...?*
Sigue todo recto	*Go straight on*
Gira ...	*Turn ...*
a la derecha	*right*
a la izquierda	*left*
Toma la ...	*Take the ...*
primera / segunda / tercera	*first / second / third*
calle a la derecha	*road on the right*
calle a la izquierda	*road on the left*
Pasa ...	*Go over ...*
el puente / los semáforos	*the bridge / traffic lights*
Está ...	*It is ...*
cerca	*near*
lejos	*far*
enfrente de (la piscina)	*opposite (the swimming pool)*

Had a look ☐ Nearly there ☐ Nailed it ☐

¿Cómo es tu zona? / *What is your area like?*

Está situado/a ...	*It is situated ...*
en un valle	*in a valley*
al lado del río	*by the river*
al lado del mar	*by the sea*
Está rodeado/a de sierra / volcanes	*It is surrounded by mountains / volcanoes*
entre	*between*
el desierto	*the desert*
los bosques	*the woods*
las selvas subtropicales	*subtropical forests*
los lagos	*lakes*
Tiene ...	*It has ...*
un paisaje impresionante	*an impressive landscape*
lo mejor de una ciudad	*the best things of a city*

Had a look ☐ Nearly there ☐ Nailed it ☐

El clima es ...	*The climate is ...*
soleado / seco / frío / variable	*sunny / dry / cold / variable*
Llueve a menudo.	*It rains often.*
Hay mucha marcha.	*There is lots going on.*
Es ...	*It is ...*
mi ciudad natal	*my home town*
mi lugar favorito	*my favourite place*
famoso/a por ...	*famous for ...*
un paraíso	*a paradise*

Had a look ☐ Nearly there ☐ Nailed it ☐

Módulo 5 Palabras

Se puede …	You / One can …	El último día	On the last day
pasar mucho tiempo al aire libre	spend lots of time in the open air	Si …	If …
apreciar la naturaleza	appreciate nature	hace sol	it's sunny
subir a la torre	go up the tower	hace calor	it's hot
disfrutar de las vistas	enjoy the views	hace mal tiempo	it's bad weather
alquilar bolas de agua	hire water balls	hace viento	it's windy
Se pueden …	You / One can …	llueve	it rains
practicar ciclismo y senderismo	do cycling and hiking	hay chubascos	there are showers
probar platos típicos	try local dishes	¡Qué bien!	How great!
practicar deportes acuáticos	do water sports	¡Qué guay!	How cool!
		¡Buena idea!	Good idea!
		De acuerdo.	OK.

Had a look ☐ Nearly there ☐ Nailed it ☐

Had a look ☐ Nearly there ☐ Nailed it ☐

En la oficina de turismo / At the tourist office

¿Tiene …?	Do you have …?
más información sobre la excursión a …	more information about the trip to …
un plano de la ciudad	a map of the town / city
¿Cuándo abre …?	When does … open?
¿Cuánto cuesta una entrada?	How much is a ticket?
para adultos	for adults
para niños	for children
¿Dónde se pueden comprar las entradas?	Where can you buy tickets?
¿A qué hora sale el autobús?	What time does the bus leave?
cada media hora	every half an hour

Las tiendas / Shops

el banco	bank
el estanco	tobacconist's
la carnicería	butcher's
la estación de trenes	train station
la frutería	greengrocer's
la joyería	jeweller's
la librería	book shop
la panadería	bakery
la pastelería	cake shop
la peluquería	hairdresser's
la pescadería	fish shop
la zapatería	shoe shop
sellos	stamps
horario comercial	hours of business
de lunes a viernes	from Monday to Friday
abre a la(s) …	it opens at …
cierra a la(s) …	it closes at …
no cierra a mediodía	it doesn't close at midday
cerrado domingo y festivos	closed on Sundays and public holidays
abierto todos los días	open every day

Had a look ☐ Nearly there ☐ Nailed it ☐

Had a look ☐ Nearly there ☐ Nailed it ☐

¿Qué harás mañana? / What will you do tomorrow?

Visitaré la catedral.	I will visit the cathedral.
Sacaré muchas fotos.	I will take lots of photos.
Subiré al teleférico.	I will go up the cable car.
Nadaré en el mar.	I will swim in the sea.
Descansaré en la playa.	I will relax on the beach.
Iré al polideportivo.	I will go to the sports centre.
Jugaré al bádminton.	I will play badminton.
Haré una excursión en barco / autobús.	I will go on a boat / bus trip.
Veré delfines.	I will see dolphins.
Iré de compras.	I will go shopping.
Compraré regalos.	I will buy presents.

Recuerdos y regalos / Souvenirs and presents

¿Me puede ayudar?	Can you help me?
Quiero comprar …	I want to buy …
el abanico	fan
el llavero	key ring
el oso de peluche	teddy bear
los pendientes	earrings
la gorra	cap
las pegatinas	stickers
Es para …	It is for …
¿Tiene uno/a más barato/a?	Do you have a cheaper one?
¿Cuánto es?	How much is it?

Had a look ☐ Nearly there ☐ Nailed it ☐

El primer día	On the first day
El segundo día	On the second day
Otro día	Another day

Módulo 5 Palabras

Quejas — *Complaints*

Quiero devolver …	I want to return …
Está roto/a.	It is broken.
Es demasiado estrecho/a.	It is too tight.
Es demasiado largo/a.	It is too long.
Tiene un agujero.	It has a hole.
Tiene una mancha.	It has a stain.
¿Puede reembolsarme?	Can you reimburse me?
Podemos hacer un cambio.	We can exchange (it).
Aquí tiene el recibo.	Here is the receipt.
¿Qué me recomienda?	What do you recommend?
¿Qué tal …?	How about …?
¿Qué te parece(n) …?	What do you think of …?
¿Me puedo probar …?	Can I try on …?
una talla más grande	a bigger size
Me lo/la/los/las llevo.	I'll take it / them.

Had a look ☐ Nearly there ☐ Nailed it ☐

¿Te gusta ir de compras? — *Do you like going shopping?*

(No) me gusta ir de compras.	I (don't) like going shopping.
Normalmente voy …	Usually I go …
Suelo ir …	I tend to go …
al centro comercial	to the shopping centre
Prefiero / Odio comprar …	I prefer / I hate buying …
en grandes almacenes	in department stores
en tiendas de moda	in fashion shops
en tiendas de segunda mano	in second-hand shops
en tiendas de diseño	in designer shops
en línea	online
por Internet	on the internet

Had a look ☐ Nearly there ☐ Nailed it ☐

porque …	because …
es muy divertido	it's a lot of fun
es mucho más cómodo	it's much more convenient
hay más variedad	there's more variety
puedes encontrar gangas	you can find bargains
se puede comprar de todo	you can buy everything
la ropa alternativa	alternative clothing
artículos de marca	branded items
hacer cola	to queue
esperar	to wait

Had a look ☐ Nearly there ☐ Nailed it ☐

Los pros y los contras de mi ciudad — *The pros and cons of my town/city*

Lo mejor de mi ciudad es que …	The best thing about my city is that …
hay tantas diversiones	there are so many things to do
el transporte público es muy bueno	the public transport is very good
las tiendas están tan cerca	the shops are so close
hay muchas posibilidades de trabajo	there are lots of job opportunities
Lo peor es que …	The worst thing is that …
es tan ruidoso/a	it's so noisy
hay tanto tráfico	there is so much traffic
hay tantas fábricas	there are so many factories
hay pocos espacios verdes	there are few green spaces

Had a look ☐ Nearly there ☐ Nailed it ☐

En el campo …	In the countryside …
la vida es más relajada	life is more relaxed
no hay tanta industria	there's not as much industry
hay bastante desempleo	there is quite a lot of unemployment
la red de transporte público no es fiable	the public transport network is not reliable
no hay tantos atascos	there are not as many traffic jams
Necesitamos más …	We need more …
zonas verdes	green spaces
zonas peatonales	pedestrian zones
rutas para bicis	cycleways

Had a look ☐ Nearly there ☐ Nailed it ☐

Destino Arequipa — *Destination Arequipa*

Vi sitios de interés.	I saw some sights.
Hicimos una visita guiada.	We did a guided tour.
Visité el centro a pie.	I visited the centre on foot.
Alquilé una bici de montaña.	I hired a mountain bike.
Subí a …	I went up to …
Aprendí mucho.	I learned a lot.
Comí pollo y patatas.	I ate chicken and potatoes.

Had a look ☐ Nearly there ☐ Nailed it ☐

Probé el rocoto relleno.	I tried stuffed peppers.
Había vistas maravillosas.	There were amazing views.
La ciudad era muy acogedora.	The city was very welcoming.
La gente era abierta.	The people were open.
La comida estaba muy buena.	The food was very good.
Me gustó (el clima).	I liked (the climate).
No me gustaron (los taxis).	I didn't like (the taxis).
¡Qué miedo!	What a scare!
Volveré algún día.	I will go back some day.
Visitaré otras ciudades.	I will visit other cities.
Iré a (Trujillo).	I will go to (Trujillo).

Had a look ☐ Nearly there ☐ Nailed it ☐

Extra words I should know for reading and listening activities

De compras	*Shopping*
los accesorios para mascotas	*pet accessories*
la bufanda	*scarf*
los calcetines	*socks*
la camisa	*shirt*
la camiseta	*t-shirt*
el chándal	*tracksuit*
el cinturón	*belt*
la corbata	*tie*
la falda	*skirt*
los guantes	*gloves*
los muebles	*furniture*
el pantalón corto	*shorts*
las sandalias	*sandals*
los vaqueros	*jeans*
el vestido	*dress*
las zapatillas de deporte	*trainers*
los zapatos	*shoes*

Had a look ☐ **Nearly there** ☐ **Nailed it** ☐

el cambio	*change / exchange*
el descuento	*discount*
la juguetería	*toy shop*
la papelería	*stationery shop*
la planta	*floor*
la tienda de comestibles	*grocery shop*
las rebajas	*sales*
la tarjeta de crédito	*credit card*
el/la vendedor(a)	*sales assistant*
comprar por Internet	*to shop on the internet*
estar de moda	*to be fashionable*
gastar	*to spend money / to use (energy)*
regalar	*to give a present*
vender	*to sell*
vestirse	*to get dressed / to dress*

Had a look ☐ **Nearly there** ☐ **Nailed it** ☐

Las ciudades y el campo	*Cities and the countryside*
aburrirse	*to get bored*
las áreas de ocio	*leisure areas*
el barrio	*neighbourhood*
la calle	*street*
el Casco Viejo	*the old town*
la cordillera	*mountain range*
la cueva	*cave*
el espacio	*space*
la mezquita	*mosque*
el paraíso	*paradise*
el parque infantil	*playground*
el pico	*peak*
el pie del volcán	*the foot of the volcano*
sucio/a	*dirty*

Had a look ☐ **Nearly there** ☐ **Nailed it** ☐

Otras expresiones y palabras	*Other expressions and words*
el año sabático	*gap year*
cómodo/a*	*comfortable / convenient*
el folleto	*brochure*
genial	*great*
llegar	*to arrive*
un montón de	*a lot of*
la niebla	*fog*
la nube	*cloud*
pasarlo bomba**	*to have a great time*
recibir	*to receive*
superrápido/a	*very fast*

Had a look ☐ **Nearly there** ☐ **Nailed it** ☐

Módulo 5 Palabras

M 5

⭐ ***Watch out for words that have more than one meaning**
Use the context to get the correct meaning of some words that have more than one meaning. The adjective *cómodo/a* can mean 'comfortable' or 'convenient'. Look at the following sentences: *Odio mi uniforme porque no es muy cómodo.* I hate my uniform because it isn't very comfortable. *Prefiero comprar por Internet porque es más cómodo.* I prefer to shop on the internet because it's more convenient.

⭐ ****Try to work out the meaning of words you don't know**
When trying to work out the meaning of a phrase look for clues. In the sentence, *Lo pasamos bomba, ya que hizo mucho sol y calor*, you know from the verb ending that the subject is 'we', you could conclude that whatever happened was probably good because the sun was shining, and you could guess (correctly) that *bomba* means 'bomb'. Using all that information you could arrive at the correct translation – 'We had a great time'.

Words I should know for speaking and writing activities

Las comidas	*Meals*
el desayuno	*breakfast*
la comida / el almuerzo	*lunch*
la merienda	*tea (meal)*
la cena	*dinner / evening meal*
desayunar	*to have breakfast / to have ... for breakfast*
comer	*to have lunch / to have ... for lunch*
merendar	*to have tea / to have ... for tea*
cenar	*to have dinner / to have ... for dinner*
tomar	*to have (food / drink)*

Had a look ☐ Nearly there ☐ Nailed it ☐

Desayuno ...	*I have breakfast ...*
temprano / tarde	*early / late*
a las ocho (y media)	*at (half past) eight*
a las nueve menos cuarto	*at quarter to nine*
a las nueve y cuarto	*at quarter past nine*
Desayuno ...	*For breakfast I have ...*
Como ...	*For lunch I have ...*
Meriendo ...	*For tea I have ...*
Ceno ...	*For dinner I have ...*
algo dulce / rápido	*something sweet / quick*

Had a look ☐ Nearly there ☐ Nailed it ☐

un huevo	*an egg*
un yogur	*a yogurt*
un pastel	*a cake*
un bocadillo	*a sandwich*
una hamburguesa	*a hamburger*
(el) bistec	*steak*
(el) café / (el) té	*coffee / tea*
(el) chorizo	*spicy chorizo sausage*
(el) marisco	*seafood*
(el) pescado	*fish*
(el) pollo	*chicken*
(el) zumo de naranja	*orange juice*

Had a look ☐ Nearly there ☐ Nailed it ☐

(la) carne	*meat*
(la) ensalada	*salad*
(la) fruta	*fruit*
(la) leche	*milk*
(la) sopa	*soup*
(la) tortilla	*omelette*
(los) cereales	*cereals*
(los) churros	*fried doughnut sticks*

(las) galletas	*biscuits*
(las) patatas fritas	*chips*
(las) tostadas	*toast*
(las) verduras	*vegetables*

Had a look ☐ Nearly there ☐ Nailed it ☐

Soy alérgico/a a ...	*I'm allergic to ...*
Soy vegetariano/a.	*I'm a vegetarian.*
Soy goloso/a.	*I have a sweet tooth.*
(No) tengo hambre.	*I'm (not) hungry.*
Es / Son ...	*It is / They are ...*
picante(s) / rápido/a(s)	*spicy / quick*
rico/a(s) / sano/a(s)	*tasty / healthy*

Had a look ☐ Nearly there ☐ Nailed it ☐

Las expresiones de cantidad	*Expressions of quantity*
cien gramos de ...	*100 grammes of ...*
quinientos gramos de ...	*500 grammes of ...*
un kilo (y medio) de ...	*a kilo (and a half) of ...*
un litro de ...	*a litre of ...*
un paquete de ...	*a packet of ...*
una barra de ...	*a loaf of ...*
una botella de ...	*a bottle of ...*
una caja de ...	*a box of ...*
una docena de ...	*a dozen ...*
una lata de ...	*a tin / can of ...*

Had a look ☐ Nearly there ☐ Nailed it ☐

Mi plato favorito	*My favourite dish*
Me gustaría probar ...	*I would like to try ...*
Es un tipo de comida / bebida / postre.	*It's a type of food / drink / dessert.*
Es un plato caliente / frío.	*It's a hot / cold dish.*
Es un plato típico de ...	*It's a typical dish from ...*
Contiene / Contienen ...	*It contains / They contain ...*

Had a look ☐ Nearly there ☐ Nailed it ☐

(el) aceite de oliva	*olive oil*
(el) agua	*water*
(el) ajo	*garlic*
(el) arroz	*rice*
(el) azúcar	*sugar*
(el) pan	*bread*
(el) queso	*cheese*
(la) cerveza	*beer*
(la) carne de cerdo	*pork*
(la) carne de cordero	*lamb*

Módulo 6 Palabras

(la) carne de ternera	beef
(la) coliflor	cauliflower
(la) harina	flour
(la) mantequilla	butter
(la) pasta	pasta

Had a look ☐ **Nearly there** ☐ **Nailed it** ☐

(los) guisantes	peas
(los) pepinos	cucumbers
(los) pimientos	peppers
(los) plátanos	bananas
(los) refrescos	fizzy drinks
(los) tomates	tomatoes
(las) cebollas	onions
(las) judías (verdes)	(green) beans
(las) manzanas	apples
(las) naranjas	oranges
(las) salchichas	sausages
(las) zanahorias	carrots

Had a look ☐ **Nearly there** ☐ **Nailed it** ☐

Mi rutina diaria — My daily routine

me despierto	I wake up
me levanto	I get up
me ducho	I have a shower
me afeito	I have a shave
me visto	I get dressed
me lavo los dientes	I clean my teeth
me acuesto	I go to bed
salgo de casa	I leave home
vuelvo a casa	I return home
si tengo tiempo	if I have time
enseguida	straight away
el comedor	the dining room
el cuarto de baño	the bathroom
el salón	the living room
la cocina	the kitchen
mi dormitorio	my bedroom

Had a look ☐ **Nearly there** ☐ **Nailed it** ☐

¿Qué le pasa? — What's the matter?

No me encuentro bien.	I don't feel well.
Estoy enfermo/a.	I am ill.
Estoy cansado/a.	I am tired.
Tengo calor / frío.	I am hot / cold.
Tengo un resfriado.	I have a cold.
Tengo dolor de garganta.	I have a sore throat.
Tengo fiebre.	I have a fever / temperature.
Tengo mucho sueño.	I am very sleepy.
Tengo tos.	I have a cough.
Tengo una insolación.	I have sunstroke.
Me duele(n) …	My … hurt(s).
Me he cortado …	I've cut my …
Me he quemado …	I've burnt my …
Me he roto …	I've broken my …

Had a look ☐ **Nearly there** ☐ **Nailed it** ☐

el brazo	arm
el estómago	stomach
el pie	foot
la boca	mouth
la cabeza	head
la espalda	back
la garganta	throat
la mano	hand
la nariz	nose
la pierna	leg
los dientes / las muelas	teeth
los oídos / las orejas	ears
los ojos	eyes

Had a look ☐ **Nearly there** ☐ **Nailed it** ☐

¿Desde hace cuánto tiempo?	How long for?
Desde hace …	For …
un día / un mes	a day / a month
una hora / una semana	an hour / a week
quince días	a fortnight
más de …	more than …
Tiene(s) que / Hay que …	You have to …
beber mucha agua	drink lots of water
descansar	rest
ir al hospital	go to the hospital
ir al médico	go to the doctor
ir al dentista	go to the dentist
tomar aspirinas	take aspirins
tomar este jarabe / estas pastillas	take this syrup / these tablets

Had a look ☐ **Nearly there** ☐ **Nailed it** ☐

Las fiestas — Festivals

Celebramos / Celebran la fiesta de …	We / They celebrate the festival of …
Comemos / Comen …	We / They eat …
Corremos / Corren …	We / They run …
Decoramos / Decoran las tumbas.	We / They decorate the graves.
Hacemos / Hacen hogueras.	We / They make bonfires.
Lanzamos / Lanzan huevos.	We / They throw eggs.
Llevamos / Llevan un disfraz.	We / They wear a costume.
Participamos / Participan en …	We / They participate in …

M6

Módulo 6 Palabras

Quemamos / Queman las figuras.	We / They burn the figures.
Vamos / Van a …	We / They go to …
Vemos / Ven los desfiles / los fuegos artificiales.	We / They watch the processions / the fireworks.
Es una fiesta para niños / familias / todos.	It's a festival for children / families / everyone.

Had a look ☐ Nearly there ☐ Nailed it ☐

Un día especial / *A special day*

Ayer fue …	Yesterday was …
(el) Domingo de Pascua	Easter Sunday
(la) Nochebuena	Christmas Eve
(la) Nochevieja	New Year's Eve
Comí doce uvas.	I ate twelve grapes.
Desayuné.	I had breakfast.
Recé.	I prayed.
Fui a la iglesia / a la mezquita.	I went to church / to the mosque.
Recibí regalos y tarjetas.	I received gifts and cards.
Visité a amigos.	I visited friends.
Me bañé.	I had a bath.
Me vestí.	I got dressed.
Me desperté temprano.	I woke up early.
Cantamos villancicos.	We sang carols.
Cenamos bacalao / pavo.	We had cod / turkey for dinner.
Hicimos una cena especial.	We had a special (evening) meal.
Nos acostamos muy tarde.	We went to bed very late.

Had a look ☐ Nearly there ☐ Nailed it ☐

¿Qué va a tomar? / *What are you going to have?*

Quiero reservar una mesa.	I want to book a table.
De primer plato …	For starter …
De segundo plato …	For main course …
De postre …	For dessert …
voy a tomar …	I'm going to have …
(el) filete de cerdo	pork fillet
(el) flan	crème caramel
(el) jamón serrano	Serrano ham
(el) melocotón	peach
(la) piña	pineapple
(la) tortilla de champiñones	mushroom omelette
(los) calamares	squid
(las) albóndigas	meatballs
(las) chuletas de cordero	lamb chops
(las) croquetas de atún	tuna croquettes
(las) fresas	strawberries
(las) gambas al ajillo	garlic prawns

Had a look ☐ Nearly there ☐ Nailed it ☐

¿Qué me recomienda?	What do you recommend?
El menú del día	The set menu
La especialidad de la casa	The house speciality
Está buenísimo/a / riquísimo/a.	It's extremely good / tasty.
¡Que aproveche!	Enjoy your meal!
¿Algo más?	Anything else?
Nada más, gracias.	Nothing else, thank you.
¿Me trae la cuenta, por favor?	Can you bring me the bill, please?
Me hace falta un cuchillo / un tenedor / una cuchara.	I need a knife / a fork / a spoon.
No hay aceite / sal / vinagre.	There's no oil / salt / vinegar.
El plato / vaso … está sucio / roto.	The plate / glass … is dirty / broken
El vino está malo.	The wine is bad / off.
La carne está fría.	The meat is cold.
El ambiente era alegre.	The atmosphere was cheerful / happy.
El camarero / La camarera era amable.	The waiter / waitress was nice.
El servicio era lento.	The service was slow.
Todo estaba muy limpio.	Everything was very clean.

Had a look ☐ Nearly there ☐ Nailed it ☐

Un festival de música / *A music festival*

Admiro …	I admire …
No aguanto / soporto …	I can't stand …
su comportamiento	his/her behaviour
su forma de vestir	his/her way of dressing
su talento	his/her talent
Su música / voz es …	His/her music / voice is …
Sus canciones / letras son …	His/her songs / lyrics are …
imaginativo/a(s)	imaginative
precioso/a(s)	beautiful
repetitivo/a(s)	repetitive
original(es)	original
Acabo de (pasar cuatro días)	I have just (spent four days)
Vi / Comí / Bebí / Canté / Bailé	I saw / ate / drank / sang / danced
Antes de …	Before …
Después de …	After …
Fue una experiencia inolvidable.	It was an unforgettable experience.
La próxima vez voy a …	Next time I'm going to …

Had a look ☐ Nearly there ☐ Nailed it ☐

Módulo 6 Palabras

Extra words I should know for reading and listening activities

Días y ocasiones especiales	**Special days and occasions**
el Año Nuevo	New Year
el árbol de Navidad	Christmas tree
el Día de Muertos	All Souls' Day
el Día de Reyes	Epiphany / 6 January
el día festivo	public holiday
la feria	fair
Navidad	Christmas
la Pascua	Easter
los Reyes Magos	the Three Kings
la Semana Santa	Easter week
Todos los Santos	All Saints' Day
la Tomatina	tomato throwing festival

Had a look ☐ Nearly there ☐ Nailed it ☐

Las fiestas	**Festivals**
el baile	dance
los bailarines / las bailarinas	dancers
la bruja	witch
la calabaza	pumpkin
la calavera	skull
el cartón	cardboard
la crema solar	sun cream
el espectáculo	show
la estrella	star
las gafas de sol	sunglasses
la gorra	cap
la hoguera	bonfire

Had a look ☐ Nearly there ☐ Nailed it ☐

la linterna	lantern
el pañuelo	neck scarf / handkerchief
los tapones para los oídos	ear plugs
la vela	candle
acampar	to camp
jugar a truco o trato	to play trick or treat
montar una tienda	to put up a tent
rezar	to pray

acompañados/as de	accompanied by
gratuito/a	free

Had a look ☐ Nearly there ☐ Nailed it ☐

¡A comer!	**Let's eat**
el asado de pavo	roast turkey
la copa*	wine glass
las intolerancias alimentarias	food intolerancies
la manzana de caramelo	toffee apple
la mermelada	jam
el perrito caliente	hot dog
la propina	tip
el turrón	Christmas sweet
apto/a para	suitable for
refrescante	refreshing
salado/a	savoury / salty
pedir	to order / to ask for
recomendar	to recommend
Vamos a ser ... personas.	There are going to be ... of us.
Aquí tiene otro vaso.	Here's another glass.
¡Qué asco!	How disgusting!

Had a look ☐ Nearly there ☐ Nailed it ☐

Otras palabras y frases útiles	**Other useful words and phrases**
el cuerpo	body
la iluminación	lighting
el lavavajillas	dishwasher
la ropa interior	underwear
llevar retraso	to be delayed
sacar algo del bolsillo	to take something out of your pocket
sonar	to ring
tener suerte	to be lucky
cansadísimo/a**	very tired
disponible	available
raro/a	strange
suave	soft
triste	sad

Had a look ☐ Nearly there ☐ Nailed it ☐

⭐ ***Watch out for words that have more than one meaning**

Use the context to get the correct meaning of some words that have more than one meaning, for example:
*Mi equipo favorito ganó **la copa**.* My favourite team won **the cup**.
*No voy a poner **las copas** en el lavavajillas.* I'm not going to put the **wine glasses** in the dishwasher.

⭐ ****How to make adjectives stronger**

To say 'really' tired etc. add *–ísimo* to the end of the adjective and make it agree. If the adjective ends in a vowel, remove the vowel before adding the ending, so, for example, *cansado/a* becomes *cansadísimo/a*, e.g.: *Esta niña está cansadísma.* This girl is very tired.

M 6

Módulo 7 Palabras

Words I should know for speaking and writing activities

¿En qué trabajas? / What is your job?

Trabajo en …	I work in …
un hotel / un instituto	a hotel / a school
un taller / una oficina	a garage / an office
una tienda / una peluquería	a shop / a hair salon
Ayudo a los pasajeros / los clientes.	I help the passengers / the customers.
Corto el pelo a los clientes.	I cut customers' hair.
Cuido los jardines / a los pacientes.	I look after the gardens / the patients.
Enseño a los niños.	I teach (the) children.
Hago entrevistas.	I do interviews.
Preparo platos distintos.	I prepare different dishes.
Reparo coches.	I repair cars.
Sirvo comida y bebida.	I serve food and drink.
Vendo ropa.	I sell clothes.
Es aburrido / interesante / fácil / difícil / importante / repetitivo / variado.	It's boring / interesting / easy / difficult / important / repetitive / varied.
Soy …	I am …
Es …	He/She is …
Me gustaría ser …	I would like to be …

Had a look ☐ Nearly there ☐ Nailed it ☐

azafato/a	a flight attendant
bombero/a	a firefighter
camarero/a	a waiter/waitress
cantante	a singer
cocinero/a	a cook
dependiente/a	a shop assistant
diseñador(a)	a designer
electricista	an electrician
enfermero/a	a nurse
fontanero/a	a plumber
fotógrafo/a	a photographer
ingeniero/a	an engineer
jardinero/a	a gardener
mecánico/a	a mechanic
médico/a	a doctor
músico/a	a musician
peluquero/a	a hairdresser
periodista	a journalist
pintor(a)	a painter
policía	a police officer
profesor(a)	a teacher
recepcionista	a receptionist
socorrista	a lifeguard
soldado	a soldier
veterinario/a	a vet

Had a look ☐ Nearly there ☐ Nailed it ☐

Es un trabajo para personas sociables.	It's a job for sociable people.
Es un trabajo … artístico / manual / variado	It's a … job artistic / manual / varied
con un buen sueldo	with a good salary
con responsabilidad	with responsibility
No sé.	I don't know.
Tal vez.	Perhaps.

Had a look ☐ Nearly there ☐ Nailed it ☐

¿Qué tipo de persona eres? / What type of person are you?

Creo que soy …	I think I'm …
comprensivo/a	understanding
creativo/a	creative
fuerte	strong
inteligente	intelligent
paciente	patient
práctico/a	practical
trabajador(a)	hardworking
valiente	brave

Had a look ☐ Nearly there ☐ Nailed it ☐

¿Qué haces para ganar dinero? / What do you do to earn money?

¿Tienes un trabajo a tiempo parcial?	Do you have a part-time job?
Reparto periódicos.	I deliver newspapers.
Hago de canguro.	I babysit.
Trabajo de cajero/a.	I work as a cashier.
Ayudo en casa.	I help at home.
Cocino.	I cook.
Lavo el coche / los platos.	I wash the car / the dishes.
Paseo al perro.	I walk the dog.
Paso la aspiradora.	I do the vacuuming.
Plancho la ropa.	I iron the clothes.
Pongo y quito la mesa.	I lay and clear the table.
Lo hago …	I do it …

Had a look ☐ Nearly there ☐ Nailed it ☐

antes / después del insti	before / after school
cuando necesito dinero	when I need money
los sábados	on Saturdays
todos los días	every day
una vez / dos veces a la semana	once / twice a week
Gano … euros / libras a la hora / a la semana.	I earn … euros / pounds an hour / a week.
No gano nada.	I don't earn anything.

Módulo 7 Palabras

Tengo que lavar los platos.	I have to wash the dishes.
Suelo trabajar los lunes.	I tend to work on Mondays.
(No) me gusta mi jefe/a.	I (don't) like my boss.
Mis compañeros son amables.	My colleagues are nice.
El horario es flexible.	The hours are flexible.

Had a look ☐ Nearly there ☐ Nailed it ☐

Mis prácticas laborales — Work experience

Hice mis prácticas laborales en …	I did my work experience in …
un polideportivo	a sports centre
una agencia de viajes	a travel agency
una granja	a farm
una escuela	a school
una fábrica	a factory
una tienda benéfica	a charity shop
la empresa de mi madre	my mum's company

Had a look ☐ Nearly there ☐ Nailed it ☐

Arreglé los estantes / los folletos.	I tidied the shelves / the brochures.
Atendí a los clientes.	I served the customers.
Ayudé en las clases de educación física.	I helped in PE classes.
Contesté el teléfono.	I answered the phone.
Di clases de natación.	I gave swimming lessons.
Escribí cartas.	I wrote letters.
Hice reservas.	I made reservations.
Mandé correos electrónicos.	I sent emails.
Pinté y leí libros.	I painted and read books.
Saqué fotocopias.	I did photocopying.
Trabajé en el gimnasio.	I worked in the gym.
Vendí ropa.	I sold clothes.
Me encantó.	I loved it.
Me gustó (mucho).	I (really) liked it.
No me gustó (nada).	I didn't like it (at all).

Had a look ☐ Nearly there ☐ Nailed it ☐

Fue …	It was …
divertido / interesante / útil / una experiencia positiva / aburrido / duro / repetitivo / una pérdida de tiempo	fun / interesting / useful / a positive experience / boring / hard work / repetitive / a waste of time
Aprendí mucho.	I learned a lot.
No aprendí nada.	I didn't learn anything.
Mi jefe / jefa era …	My boss was …
Mis compañeros eran …	My colleagues were …
Los clientes eran …	The customers were …
alegre(s)	cheerful
severo/a(s)	strict
agradable(s)	pleasant
desagradable(s)	unpleasant
educado/a(s)	polite
maleducado/a(s)	rude
El banco era moderno / antiguo.	The bank was modern / old.

Had a look ☐ Nearly there ☐ Nailed it ☐

¿Por qué aprender idiomas? — Why learn languages?

Hablo (un poco de) alemán.	I speak (a bit of) German.
árabe	Arabic
español	Spanish
francés	French
inglés	English
italiano	Italian
mandarín	Mandarin
polaco	Polish
ruso	Russian
urdu	Urdu
(No) domino el inglés.	I (don't) speak English fluently.
Estudio francés desde hace … años.	I've been studying French for … years.
Aprender un idioma te permite …	Learning a language allows you to …
descubrir nuevas culturas.	discover new cultures.
encontrar un buen trabajo.	find a good job.
hacer nuevos amigos.	make new friends.
trabajar o estudiar en el extranjero.	work or study abroad.
viajar a otros países.	travel to other countries.

Had a look ☐ Nearly there ☐ Nailed it ☐

¿Cómo vas a viajar? — How are you going to travel?

Voy a viajar en autobús / autocar / avión / tren.	I am going to travel by bus / coach / plane / train.
Lo bueno / malo es que …	The good / bad thing is that …
Lo mejor es que …	The best thing is that …
es barato / cómodo / rápido.	it's cheap / comfortable / quick.
hay poco tráfico en las autopistas.	there isn't much traffic on the motorways.
Puedes …	You can …
ver películas mientras viajas.	watch films whilst you travel.

M7

Módulo 7 Palabras

dejar tu maleta en la consigna.	leave your suitcase in the left-luggage office.
Lo peor es esperar en la parada de autobús.	The worst thing is waiting at the bus stop.

Had a look ☐ **Nearly there** ☐ **Nailed it** ☐

Viajando en tren / Travelling by train

Quisiera un billete de ida a …	I would like a single ticket to …
Quisiera un billete de ida y vuelta a …	I would like a return ticket to …
¿De qué andén sale?	From which platform does it leave?
¿A qué hora sale?	What time does it leave?
¿A qué hora llega?	What time does it arrive?
¿Es directo o hay que cambiar?	Is it direct or do I have to change?
el tren con destino a … sale de la vía / del andén dos.	the train to … leaves from platform two.
el tren AVE	high-speed train
la taquilla	the ticket office

Had a look ☐ **Nearly there** ☐ **Nailed it** ☐

Solicitando un trabajo / Applying for a job

Muy señor mío	Dear Sir
Le escribo para solicitar el puesto de …	I'm writing to apply for the post of …
Le adjunto mi currículum vitae.	I'm enclosing my CV.
Le agradezco su amable atención.	Thank you for your kind attention.
Atentamente	Yours sincerely / faithfully
He ayudado (en una escuela).	I've helped (in a school).
He estudiado (dos idiomas).	I've studied (two languages).
He hecho prácticas (en una oficina).	I've done work experience (in an office).
He servido comida y bebida.	I've served food and drink.
He trabajado (en equipo).	I've worked (in a team).
Me interesa este trabajo porque …	I'm interested in this job because …
tengo buen sentido del humor.	I have a good sense of humour.
me encanta trabajar con …	I love working with …

Had a look ☐ **Nearly there** ☐ **Nailed it** ☐

El futuro / The future

Espero …	I hope to …
Me gustaría …	I would like to …
Quiero …	I want to …
Voy a …	I am going to …
aprender a conducir	learn to drive
aprobar mis exámenes	pass my exams
buscar un trabajo	look for a job
casarme	get married
tener hijos	have children
trabajar como voluntario/a	work as a volunteer
El matrimonio …	Marriage …
El paro …	Unemployment …
La familia …	Family …
La independencia	Independence …
Sacar buenas notas …	Getting good grades …
es esencial	is essential
es importante	is important
es preocupante	is worrying
es algo especial	is something special
es un gran problema	is a big problem

Had a look ☐ **Nearly there** ☐ **Nailed it** ☐

Me gusta ayudar a otras personas.	I like helping other people.
Me encantan los niños.	I love children.
Si …	If …
saco buenas notas	I get good grades
tengo dinero	I have money
tengo éxito	I'm successful
tengo suerte	I'm lucky
trabajo mucho	I work a lot
me caso	I get married
encontraré un trabajo como …	I will find a job as …
compartiré piso con …	I will share a flat with …
compraré un coche	I will buy a car
haré el bachillerato	I will do A Levels
iré a la universidad	I will go to university
seré rico/a y famoso/a	I will be rich and famous
tendré hijos	I will have children

Had a look ☐ **Nearly there** ☐ **Nailed it** ☐

Un año sabático / A gap year

Me tomaré un año sabático.	I will take a gap year.
Ayudaré a construir un colegio.	I will help to build a school.
Haré un viaje en Interrail por Europa.	I will go Interrailing around Europe.
Mejoraré mi nivel de inglés.	I will improve my level of English.
Pasaré un año en Latinoamérica.	I will spend a year in Latin America.
Trabajaré en un proyecto medioambiental.	I will work on an environmental project.
Viajaré por el mundo.	I will travel around the world.

Had a look ☐ **Nearly there** ☐ **Nailed it** ☐

Módulo 7 Palabras

Extra words I should know for reading and listening activities

Verbos útiles / Useful verbs

aprovechar*	to make the most of
archivar documentos	to file documents
conseguir un título en algo	to get a qualification in something
estar harto/a de	to be fed up with
funcionar	to work (machine)
llamar por teléfono	to telephone
llegar a ser	to become
obtener	to get / to obtain
ordeñar las vacas	to milk the cows
vigilar a alguien	to supervise someone

Had a look ☐ Nearly there ☐ Nailed it ☐

El mundo laboral / The working world

la asignatura	subject
la cita	appointment
el comercio	commerce / trade
la construcción	building (act of)
las cualidades	qualities
el curso de formación profesional	vocational course
el/la ejecutivo/a	executive
el/la empleado/a	employee
el empleo	employment

Had a look ☐ Nearly there ☐ Nailed it ☐

la experiencia previa	previous experience
las habilidades lingüísticas	language skills
las horas de trabajo flexibles	flexitime
el objetivo	aim / objective
el periodismo	journalism
el permiso de conducir	driving licence
el requisito	requirement
la revista de moda	fashion magazine
la sanidad**	public health
las tareas en casa	housework
el teletrabajo	work from home
deseable	desirable
laboral	working
monótono/a	monotonous

Had a look ☐ Nearly there ☐ Nailed it ☐

Los trabajos / Jobs

el/la animador(a)	activities organiser
el bailarín / la bailarina	dancer
el hombre / la mujer de negocios	businessman / businesswoman
el/la modelo	model
el/la obrero/a	worker
el/la operario/a	operator
el/la socorrista	lifeguard
el/la traductor(a)	translator

Had a look ☐ Nearly there ☐ Nailed it ☐

Otras palabras útiles / Other useful words

el/la cerdo/a	pig
el destino	destination (train timetable)
la emisora de radio	radio station
el entorno	surroundings
el/la granjero/a	farmer
el lavaplatos	dishwasher
la llegada	arrival time (train timetable)
el/la mochilero/a	backpacker
el restaurante de comida rápida	fast food restaurant
la salida	departure time (train timetable)
la vida nocturna	night life
cariñoso/a	affectionate

Had a look ☐ Nearly there ☐ Nailed it ☐

M 7

⭐ ***Try to work out meanings of unfamiliar verbs**
You may have heard the expression ¡Que aproveche! (Enjoy your meal! – or in other words, 'Make the most of your meal'). If you have, it will make it easier for you to work out what aprovechar means in other contexts, for example: Me gustaría aprovechar el año para hacer algo útil. I'd like to make the most of the year to do something useful.

⭐ ****Don't jump to conclusions**
Watch out for false friends – la sanidad doesn't mean 'sanity', it means 'public health'. The secret is to look at the word in context. And remember, you can always consult a dictionary when you come across new words to make absolutely sure what they mean.

Módulo 8 Palabras

Words I should know for speaking and writing activities

¿Cómo es tu casa?	What is your house like?
Vivo en …	I live in …
un bloque de pisos	a block of flats
una casa individual	a detached house
una casa adosada	a semi-detached / terraced house
un piso	a flat
un apartamento	an apartment
una granja	a farmhouse
Está en …	It is in …
el centro de la ciudad	the centre of the city
un barrio en las afueras	a district in the suburbs
las afueras	the outskirts / suburbs
el campo	the country
un pueblo en la costa	a village on the coast
la montaña	the mountains

Had a look ☐ Nearly there ☐ Nailed it ☐

abajo / arriba	downstairs / upstairs
en la planta baja	on the ground floor
en la primera planta	on the first floor
en el primer piso	on the first floor
fuera …	outside …
hay …	there is …
un aseo	a toilet
un comedor	a dining room
un cuarto de baño	a bathroom
un despacho / un estudio	a study
un dormitorio	a bedroom
un salón	a living room
un garaje	a garage
un jardín	a garden
una cocina	a kitchen
una terraza	a terrace / a balcony
una mesa	a table
unas sillas	some chairs

Had a look ☐ Nearly there ☐ Nailed it ☐

¿Cómo cuidas el medio ambiente en casa?	How do you look after the environment at home?
Apago / Apagamos	I turn off / We turn off
la luz	the light
la lámpara	the lamp
Desenchufo / Desenchufamos	I unplug / We unplug
los aparatos eléctricos	electric devices
el equipo de música	the stereo
el ordenador	the computer
la televisión	the television

Prefiero usar …	I prefer using …
la ducha	the shower
la bañera	the bath

Had a look ☐ Nearly there ☐ Nailed it ☐

Ahorramos agua.	We save water.
Separamos …	We separate …
Reciclamos …	We recycle …
la basura	the rubbish
el papel	paper
el plástico	plastic
el vidrio	glass
los cubos de basura	rubbish bins
Cerramos …	We shut …
las ventanas	the windows
la puerta	the door
Compramos productos verdes.	We buy green products.
el armario	the cupboard
el sofá	the sofa
la cama	the bed
la lavadora	the washing machine
la calefacción	the heating
Malgastamos energía.	We waste energy.
hacer todo lo posible	to do everything possible
ser verde	to be green

Had a look ☐ Nearly there ☐ Nailed it ☐

¿Cuál es el problema global más serio?	What is the most serious global problem?
El mayor problema global es …	The greatest global problem is …
el paro / el desempleo	unemployment
el medio ambiente	the environment
el hambre	hunger
los sin hogar / techo	the homeless
los animales en peligro de extinción	the animals in danger of extinction
la desigualdad social	social inequality
la salud	health
la crisis económica	the economic crisis
la contaminación de los ríos / mares	the pollution of the rivers / seas
la pobreza	poverty
la drogadicción	drug addiction
los drogadictos	drug addicts
los obesos	obese people
los animales amenazados	endangered animals
la tasa de desempleo	the unemployment rate

Had a look ☐ Nearly there ☐ Nailed it ☐

Módulo 8 Palabras

¡Actúa localmente! — *Act locally!*
Hay demasiada basura. — *There is too much rubbish.*
El aire está contaminado. — *The air is polluted.*
la sequía — *drought*
el calentamiento global — *global warming*
la destrucción de los bosques — *destruction of woodland / forest*
Para … — *In order to …*
limpiar las calles — *clean (up) the streets*
proteger el medio ambiente — *protect the environment*
proteger los ríos y mares — *protect the rivers and seas*
reducir la contaminación — *reduce pollution*
luchar contra el calentamiento global — *combat global warming*

Had a look ☐ **Nearly there** ☐ **Nailed it** ☐

Se debería … — *You should …*
ducharse — *shower*
plantar más árboles — *plant more trees*
usar productos ecológicos — *use environmentally-friendly products*
ahorrar energía en casa — *save energy at home*
usar el transporte público — *use public transport*
reciclar todo lo posible — *recycle everything possible*
usar energías renovables — *use renewable energies*
hacer proyectos medioambientales — *do environmental projects*
apagar la luz — *switch off the light*
reciclar el papel y el vidrio — *recycle paper and glass*
desenchufar los aparatos eléctricos — *unplug electronic devices*
No se debería … — *You should not …*
tirar basura al suelo — *throw rubbish on the ground*
usar bolsas de plástico — *use plastic bags*
malgastar el agua / la energía — *waste water / energy*

Had a look ☐ **Nearly there** ☐ **Nailed it** ☐

¿Qué hay que hacer? — *What must be done?*
Hay que … — *One / We must …*
cuidar el planeta — *look after the planet*
crear más empleos — *create more jobs*
reducir el consumo — *reduce consumption*
apoyar a proyectos de ayuda — *support aid projects*
usar productos verdes — *use green products*
hacer campañas publicitarias — *do publicity campaigns*
Me quedé sin hogar — *I ended up homeless*
Perdí mi trabajo — *I lost my job*
Sufrí agresiones — *I suffered attacks*
Pasé una semana … — *I spent a week …*
Encontré un centro de ayuda — *I found a help centre*
el alquiler — *the rent*
Si tengo éxito … — *If I am successful …*
una organización humanitaria — *humanitarian organisation*
actualmente — *currently*
por ciento — *per cent*
la edad media — *average age*

Had a look ☐ **Nearly there** ☐ **Nailed it** ☐

Una dieta sana — *A healthy diet*
los alimentos — *foods*
lácteos — *milk products*
carne, pescados y huevos — *meat, fish and eggs*
frutas y verduras — *fruit and vegetables*
cereales — *cereals*
fideos — *noodles*
grasas — *fats*
dulces — *sugars / sweet things*
los nutrientes — *nutrients*
proteínas — *proteins*
minerales — *minerals*
grasa — *fat*
sal — *salt*
vitaminas — *vitamins*
azúcar — *sugar*
gluten — *gluten*

Had a look ☐ **Nearly there** ☐ **Nailed it** ☐

Llevo una dieta sana. — *I have a healthy diet.*
Mi dieta es poco variada. — *My diet is not very varied.*
Suelo comer / beber … — *I usually eat / drink …*
porque contiene(n) … — *because it contains (they contain) …*
la fibra … — *fibre …*
combate la obesidad — *combats obesity*
el sabor — *taste*
sano / malsano — *healthy / unhealthy*
No puedo … — *I can't …*
llevar una dieta sana — *have a healthy diet*
evitar la comida basura — *avoid junk food*
dormir — *sleep*
comer sano — *eat heathily*

Had a look ☐ **Nearly there** ☐ **Nailed it** ☐

porque … — *because …*
soy adicto/a a — *I'm addicted to …*
soy alérgico/a a — *I'm allergic to …*
(No) voy a … — *I'm (not) going to …*
cambiar mi dieta — *change my diet*

M 8

43

Módulo 8 Palabras

mejorar mi dieta	improve my diet
evitar comer / beber ...	avoid eating / drinking ...
comer más / menos ...	eat more / less ...
preparar comida en casa	prepare food at home
practicar más deporte	do more sport
buscar recetas en línea	look for recipes online

Had a look ☐ **Nearly there** ☐ **Nailed it** ☐

¡Vivir a tope! / *Live life to the full!*

Beber alcohol	Drinking alcohol
Fumar cigarrillos / porros	Smoking cigarettes / joints
Tomar drogas blandas / duras	Taking soft / hard drugs
Emborracharse	Getting drunk
(no) es ...	is / isn't ...
ilegal / peligroso	illegal / dangerous
una pérdida de dinero	a waste of money
una tontería	stupid
bueno / malo para la salud	good / bad for your health

Had a look ☐ **Nearly there** ☐ **Nailed it** ☐

No me parece ...	It doesn't seem ... (to me)
tan malo	so bad
porque / ya que ...	because / as ...
te relaja	it relaxes you
causa el fracaso escolar	it causes failure at school
te hace sentir ...	it makes you feel ...
bien / más adulto	good / more grown up
Es fácil engancharse.	It is easy to get hooked.
¡Qué asco!	How disgusting!
Decidí ...	I decided ...
cambiar mi vida / dieta	to change my life / diet
dejar de fumar	to give up smoking
evitar la grasa	to avoid fat
A partir de ahora	From now on

Had a look ☐ **Nearly there** ☐ **Nailed it** ☐

¿Por qué son importantes los eventos deportivos internacionales? / *Why are international sporting events important?*

los Juegos Paralímpicos	the Paralympics
los Juegos Olímpicos	the Olympics
la Copa Mundial de Fútbol	the Football World Cup
Promueven ...	They promote ...
la participación en el deporte	participation in sport
el turismo	tourism
Unen a la gente.	They unite people.
Elevan el orgullo nacional.	They increase national pride.
Transmiten los valores de respeto y disciplina.	They transmit the values of respect and discipline.

Had a look ☐ **Nearly there** ☐ **Nailed it** ☐

Una desventaja es ...	A disadvantage is ...
el riesgo de ataques terroristas	the risk of terrorist attacks
el tráfico	the traffic
el dopaje	doping
el coste de organización	the cost of organisation
los grandes acontecimientos deportivos	big sporting events
los eventos solidarios	charity events
te dan la oportunidad de ...	give you the opportunity to ...
recaudar dinero	raise money
informar a la gente	inform people
ayudar a otras personas	help other people
hacer algo práctico	do something practical
organizar un torneo / un espectáculo	organise a tournament / a show

Had a look ☐ **Nearly there** ☐ **Nailed it** ☐

Módulo 8 Palabras

Extra words I should know for reading and listening activities

Verbos útiles	*Useful verbs*
atraer	*to attract*
aumentar	*to increase*
beneficiar	*to benefit*
cultivar	*to cultivate*
dañar	*to harm / to damage*
desaparecer	*to disappear*
encender	*to turn on (lights, television)*
encontrarse bien / mal	*to feel well / ill*
faltar	*to be missing*
inquietarse	*to worry / to upset oneself*

Had a look ☐ Nearly there ☐ Nailed it ☐

inspirarse (me inspira)	*to inspire (he/she/it inspires me)*
mantenerse en forma	*to keep fit / in shape*
oler*	*to smell*
preocuparse	*to worry*
recoger basura	*to pick up litter*
respirar	*to breathe*
salvar	*to save*
sentirse seguro/a	*to feel safe*
ser rico/a en	*to be rich in*
ser solidario/a	*to be supportive / caring*
solucionar	*to solve / to resolve*
tener miedo a algo	*to be afraid of something*

Had a look ☐ Nearly there ☐ Nailed it ☐

Nombres útiles	*Useful nouns*
la carrera	*race / university course / degree / career*
el círculo vicioso	*vicious circle*
el/la compatriota	*fellow countryman/ woman*
la culpa	*fault / blame / guilt*
el daño	*harm / damage*
el/la habitante	*inhabitant*
la hostelería	*hotel industry*
el medio maratón	*half marathon*
un montón	*a lot*
los necesitados	*needy people*
el propósito	*aim / purpose / objective*
el recurso	*resource*
la red de transporte público	*public transport network*
la soledad	*loneliness*
la terraza	*terrace*
el/la vecino/a	*neighbour*

Had a look ☐ Nearly there ☐ Nailed it ☐

Adjetivos útiles	*Useful adjectives*
equilibrado/a	*balanced*
escaso/a	*scarce*
grave	*serious*
incómodo/a**	*uncomfortable*
inquietante	*worrying*
medioambiental	*environmental*
pobre	*poor*
poco sano/a	*not healthy*
preocupado/a	*worried*
preocupante	*worrying*
recargable	*rechargeable*
renovable	*renewable*
saludable	*healthy*

Had a look ☐ Nearly there ☐ Nailed it ☐

M 8

⭐ ***Learn irregular verbs**
Take time to learn useful irregular verbs. Did you know that ¡Huele mal! (It smells bad!) comes from the verb *oler* (to smell), which is irregular in the present tense?

⭐ ****How to spot opposites**
In English 'un-' is often used before an adjective to give the opposite. In Spanish to form some opposites *in-* is used in the same way, e.g. *cómodo* (comfortable) *incómodo* (uncomfortable). Some other examples are:
feliz (happy) **in***feliz* (unhappy)
fiel (faithful) **in***fiel* (unfaithful)
See if you can think of some more. You could use a dictionary to help you.

45

ISBN 978-1-292-17259-0